St. Louis Community
College

Library

5801 Wilson Avenue
St. Louis, Missouri 63110

St. Louis Community College
at Meramec

ANCHOR OF LIBERTY

C. Fred Kleinknecht

Foreword by
Warren E. Burger

THE SUPREME COUNCIL, 33°
ANCIENT AND ACCEPTED SCOTTISH RITE
OF FREEMASONRY
SOUTHERN JURISDICTION
UNITED STATES OF AMERICA
1987

ii

Dedication

To the Signers
of the United States Constitution,
our "Anchor of Liberty."

Table of Contents

Foreword

Warren E. Burger

Chairman, Commission on the Bicentennial
of the United States Constitution

Chief Justice of the United States
1969-1986

George Mason wrote in the Virginia Declaration of Rights
that if free people do not reexamine their liberties and how
they were obtained, they risk losing those rights. That is our
goal during this Bicentennial of the United States Constitution
—to reflect upon the rights the document ensures—and the
responsibilities. Every generation holds the Constitutional liberties in trust, and it is our solemn duty to pass these rights unim-
paired to "our posterity."

Among those who played key roles in securing this
Constitution were members of a patriotic brotherhood of
men—nearly one-third of the Signers were Masons. The active
involvement of such organizations is crucial to the success of
our nationwide history and civics lesson.

Introduction

This book, **Anchor of Liberty,** is a response to the challenge, "Let there be light." It comes at a time when national surveys are determining that many citizens are ignorant of the contents and substance of the great documents of American history. If used properly it could serve as a guiding light in one's study of those historical documents which produced the greatest nation on Earth. It should prove to be a valuable supplementary tool in enabling teachers and students alike to receive more light on our Nation's tumultuous beginning. **Anchor of Liberty** is worthy of a prized place in any curriculum dealing with freedom in our secondary schools and colleges.

One can find unfolding within these pages the thrilling drama of how the making of a constitution can contribute to the dramatic growth of a budding nation. The framers of this constitution spent a long, hot and frustrating summer in 1787 seeking a meeting of the minds among great men with divergent views on how liberty could best be achieved. They were determined to produce a document which would guarantee future decades a good quality of life. **Anchor of Liberty** introduces you to men who took upon themselves the arduous role of penning on parchment the spirit of the Revolution. Many of them were heroes of its famous battles who had spirits which differed, and long hours of heated debate were required in the forging of this priceless document of freedom. Many historians feel this heated controversy in overcoming their differences helps reveal to us the nature of these great men.

This book provides for us a road map for renewing our knowledge and understanding of the Articles of the Constitution and its Bill of Rights. It provides, in quotation marks, the irrevocable section of laws which provides "human dignity for every American." The Bill of Rights comes alive as the writer expresses in a language simple, yet profound, the strengths of those sections which charter the freedoms that made our Nation great. Every citizen who reads the few pages of this book devoted to the Bill of Rights should have a new appreciation for the freedom he enjoys. The Bill of Rights is truly "America's guarantee of Freedom." It is, therefore, important that no American make the tragic mistake of being ignorant of its provisions, or of being thoughtless with a lack of appreciation for its meanings.

Anchor of Liberty gives to a new generation of Americans a book which should shed additional light upon the documents of America's beginning. A clearer understanding of our heritage will enable all Americans to face the future better prepared to deal with the struggles and strife necessary in keeping America free and strong. This book which provides more light regarding our freedom documents should be a welcome addition in the classrooms of America.

H. Wallace Reid
Superintendent, Anderson City Schools
Anderson, South Carolina

Public officers are the servants and agents of the people, to execute laws which the people have made and within the limits of a constitution which they have established.

Grover Cleveland

Chapter One

Blueprint for Freedom

"LIBERTY is generally established with difficulty in the midst of storms; it is perfected by civil disorders; and its benefits cannot be appreciated until it is already old." This comment by Alexis de Tocqueville, a French admirer of early 19th century America, is even truer today than when it was written in the 1840's. This year, 1987, marks the Bicentennial of the Constitutional Convention held during the summer of 1787.

The 13 American Colonies, by then independent American states, were in the "midst of storms." Yet during the deliberations of the 55 delegates in the State House of Pennsylvania in Philadelphia, now called Independence Hall, liberty was secured for all Americans for all time. Article by article, the Constitution spelled out the proper role of government and the individual rights and responsibilities of each citizen.

It established a priceless blueprint for freedom from which would grow a strong, stable, unified nation. The conflicts of two centuries have only perfected our freedoms. Our benefits have increased. Our appreciation of what the Constitution accomplished has deepened. Now that the Constitution is 200 years old, we can better, more fully understand all it did— and is still doing—to establish, protect and perpetuate our American liberties.

In 1787, however, the situation was not so clear. America had only recently won its battle for independence. The Imperial Crown and Parliament of Great Britain had

1

insisted on the right "to bind the colonies and people of America . . . in all cases whatsoever." The long and bloody Revolutionary War proved otherwise. America would be free, whatever the cost. At Jamestown, Virginia, and Plymouth, Massachusetts, enterprising colonists formed charters and compacts. These were, in effect, elemental social contracts. Voluntarily, these early settlers chose their own representatives, empowered them to form laws for civil governance

Signing of the Constitution—*Rossiter*

and promised to abide by these laws. They rejected individual selfishness, the state of nature, for the common good of a civilized society.

Americans were not about to sacrifice their hard-won and long-established rights and liberties to a distant authority that refused them representation yet demanded obedience "in all cases whatsoever." Was there ever a blunter statement of tyranny? England may have forgotten the Magna Charta of

1215 wrung from King John by his barons and the Bill of Rights demanded by Englishmen of William and Mary in 1689, but Americans had not!

At Lexington and Concord, Trenton and Yorktown, Americans fought to defend the 169 years of virtual freedom they had enjoyed as a people. In France, Benjamin Franklin guided that nation into supporting America. At home, General George Washington was unanimously elected Commander in Chief of the Continental Army. For 8 years the battle raged. Finally and at great cost, victory was won and America was free.

We had stated the new nation's grievances and goals in the Declaration of Independence in 1776. Similarly, nearly every former colony soon thereafter called a convention to write a state constitution. Some adopted two or three in succession. Futhermore, the states were bound since 1781 in a loose union under the Articles of Confederation. Clearly, by 1787 America had developed a strong constitutional tradition. These written documents—derived from and approved by the people—expressed concepts of social contract and placed the law over individual will.

The Articles of Confederation, however, were fatally flawed. The Revolution had taught and ingrained fear of foreign domination. No state wished to risk replacing British with federal tyranny. At the heart of the problem was Article II. In it each state retained "its sovereignty, freedom, and independence." There was no real unity of people. The Articles of Confederation resulted in what was essentially a "league of friendship." In it each state had one vote in a single-chambered Congress of the United States. Congress became a sort of gathering place for ambassadors from the states.

Under the Articles, the government could not tax, print money, promote trade, raise troops or make an individual do anything. There was no direct relation of the local citizen to the central government. All significant civil power was kept by the individual states. The results were soon evident.

Lacking the ability to raise taxes, the federal government could not finance its programs. Nothing got done. Lacking a common currency, the country was swamped by worthless paper money issued by the states. Debtors escaped their just responsibilities and contracts collapsed. Lacking control of trade, commerce became blocked as individual states set up protective import and export duties. River and road transport languished. Lacking the defense of a strong national army, pioneers on the Western frontiers found themselves unprotected from the Indians, Spaniards and British. America was at the mercy of enemies both within and beyond its borders. Lacking direct control over its citizens, federal authority could not prosecute criminals or safeguard the welfare of society in general. America was fragmented and one step from anarchy.

The solution to these problems, the Constitution itself, came about in a series of small steps. Virginia and Maryland had a disagreement about control of boat traffic on the Potomac River. Despite the leadership of strong individuals such as George Washington and James Madison, settlement proved difficult. Even if Maryland and Virginia agreed, what about shipment of goods to other states? Obviously, the problem was bigger than blocked cargoes between two states. In 1786 five states were consulted. They met in Annapolis. The more they talked, the clearer it was that what the country needed was an overhaul of the entire system. Delegates to this Annapolis Convention asked Alexander Hamilton to invite representatives to a meeting in Philadelphia in May 1787. Congress was moving slowly toward the Constitutional Convention whose bicentennial we celebrate this year.

Yet the people were cautious. Only the fact that Washington, Franklin and other eminent men supported the planned convention kept the idea alive. Also, Virginia was the first state to choose delegates. By selecting Washington as its leading delegate, Virginia added to the luster of the proposed convention. In all, 11 states sent delegates to the initial meetings.

It was not a large group. Only 55 men participated. But what men! Washington, striding at the head of the Virginia delegation, brought with him James Madison, Edmund Randolph, George Mason, George Wythe, John Blair and James McClurg. Then there was Benjamin Franklin, the great harmonizer of the convention, leading the Pennsylvania delegation which included James Wilson, one of the ablest lawyers in America at the time, and Robert Morris, financial leader of the Revolution. The New York delegation included Alexander Hamilton, Revolutionary War aide of General Washington and administrative wizard. The South was represented by, among others, John Rutledge and Charles Pinckney. Most of the Convention delegates were decorated veterans of the Revolutionary War, well-educated lawyers, men of experience in government. They were America's best, a body of men well fitted to produce our Nation's greatest document, the Constitution.

They met for the first time on May 25, 1787, in the State House in Philadelphia. These were familiar surroundings for most of the Convention delegates. Earlier the buildings had been the home of the Continental Congress. Also, here they had signed the Declaration of Independence on July 4, 1776. Now, nearly 11 years later, they were again assembled for as great a work.

The first matter of business was the unanimous election of Washington to preside over the Convention. As its President, Washington could not take part in floor debates. Yet undoubtedly his leadership was strongly felt in every official meeting as well as in private conferences.

To free themselves from outside pressures, strict secrecy was preserved. Each state was to have one vote. Seven states would constitute a quorum. First of all, would the Articles of Confederation simply be revised? Or would the delegates walk along a new path? Would they draft an entirely new constitution? Most delegates had come expecting revision only. Others had a broader vision. Washington joined their camp and advised against "temporizing expedients."

A week of debate followed. Finally, the Convention, meeting as a committee of the whole, resolved that "a national government ought to be established consisting of a supreme legislative, executive, and judiciary." Here, already, was a key idea of the Constitution: that there should be a series of checks, a balancing of powers, so that no one branch of the government could dominate the other.

And there were other issues. How much authority would the federal government have? To what degree would the states retain their independence and power? How would the small and large states be represented so that each received proper recognition in all decisions? How many chambers would there be in the national legislature, Congress? What would be the role of the Executive, the President?

Thorough consideration, long debate and satisfactory compromise were the order of the day. The Constitution as it exists today is, in fact, a bundle of compromises. Still, simple political convenience did not rule. The Framers of the Constitution saw beyond the immediate needs of their day. They established a legal and political system that has weathered two centuries of war and peace, crisis and prosperity. The genius of the Founding Fathers was that they managed to devise a document that protects minorities from the possible tyranny of the majority.

For instance, Virginia's delegates, representing the large states, wanted representation in Congress by population. Delegates from New Jersey, speaking for the small states, wanted equal representation. One state: one vote. The compromise? Following the lead of the Connecticut delegates, it was agreed that the national assembly would consist of two houses. In the Senate, or upper chamber, states would be equally represented by two duly-elected officials. In the House, or lower chamber, representation would be based on population. The more citizens in a state, the more Representatives elected to express their desires.

Other issues—regulation of commerce, length of terms in

office for Senators, Representatives and the President, the appointment of federal judges—these were hammered out, little by little, as the summer wore on. Gradually, the outlines of a strong central government became clear. Congress was empowered to tax, borrow money, print currency and regulate its value. The thorny issue of states' rights was solved with surprising ease. The new government would operate not upon the states, but directly upon the people. The states were to remain semi-independent governments with their own special spheres of authority. All schemes of direct coercion on the states by the federal government were rightly deemed dangerous and futile. Two systems, state and federal, were established on parallel lines. In case of conflict, the Constitution would define respective powers. Why?

Logically, if ratified by the people as presented to them by their delegates, the Constitution would be the work not just of the states individually, but of the whole people acting together on a single issue. Thus any state law, if in conflict with the common law, the Constitution as the "supreme Law of the Land," would be unconstitutional and, therefore, invalid.

But who would interpret the Constitution? Clearly there was, of course, the Supreme Court of the United States with Justices appointed for life. Raised above contemporary political strife by their lifetime tenures, these jurists would be able to rule exclusively according to the letter and spirit of the Constitution. As Chief Justice Stone said of himself and his colleagues on the bench of the Nation's highest court: "We read its (the Constitution's) words, not as we read legislative codes which are subject to continuous revision with the changing course of events, but as the revelation of the great purposes which were intended to be achieved by the Constitution as a continuing instrument of government."

Even here, however, there was compromise. The Framers of the Constitution realized that no one can be or should be totally removed from practical considerations. According to the Constitution, Supreme Court Justices are nominated by the

President and confirmed by the Senate. Consequently, a Supreme Court Justice may be selected and approved in part because of current political considerations. Yet, as many Presidents and Senators have discovered, once on the bench of the Supreme Court most Justices rise above ideological camps and contemporary issues to interpret the Constitution within the framework of what its creators originally intended.

Once cast into words by the delegates at Philadelphia, the Constitution had to be ratified. In keeping with the fact that the document begins with "We the People," it was felt that a plan forwarded by the Virginia plan would be appropriate. The Constitution would not be ratified by existing state legislatures. They had been elected for other purposes than sanctioning a wholly new Constitution. Rather, the people's voice would be heard. According to the suggestion of the Virginia delegation, it was decided that state conventions especially chosen by the people for approving or disapproving the new Constitution would be called. Ratification by 9 states would constitute acceptance by all 13 states.

Their work done, the Philadelphia delegates signed the Constitution with "Unanimous Consent of the States present" on September 17, 1787. The draft was submitted to the existing Congress under the Articles of Confederation for consideration and, more practically, for forwarding to the constitutional conventions of the 13 states.

The Constitution was now public. Opinions clashed. Dispute raged in broadsides, pamphlets, newspapers, town meetings, churches, and country crossroads. States' rights advocates challenged those in favor of a strong federal government. Sectional partisanships flared. Professional men lined up against workers, farmers and backwoodsmen. Most of all, many people noted that the Constitution failed on one basic count. It did not contain a guarantee of the simplest human rights, specifically the freedoms of speech, press, assembly, petition and worship. Discussion raged for months, and ratification became more and more difficult as opinions became fixed.

One by one the states held conventions to debate acceptance, rejection or modification. Delaware had the honor of being the first state to vote for ratification on December 7, 1787. Quickly four other states—Pennsylvania, New Jersey, Georgia and Connecticut—gave their approval. Ratification was gaining momentum. Massachusetts was the next crucial state.

In Massachusetts, Alexander Hamilton, James Madison and John Jay wrote cogent arguments in favor of ratification. These public newsletters, later organized into the famous *Federalist Papers*, turned the tide of opposition in the North. John Marshall, unaware that later he would head the Supreme Court as Chief Justice, joined the fray. The sticking point was the failure, as already noted, of the Constitution to have an open statement of guaranteed human rights.

A compromise was worked out. It was agreed that amendments to the Constitution by the state conventions could be made, though not as conditions of ratification. They were, instead, to be strong recommendations of which the states were "convinced." Opponents pointed out that there was no assurance that the proposed amendments would become law. Proponents argued that the recommendations were so clear and basic that their acceptance was inevitable. Acting on faith that this was so, Massachusetts ratified the draft Constitution on February 6, 1788, by a close vote of 187 to 168. Prominent among the amendments proposed by the Massachusetts convention was a bill of rights which spelled out the essential freedoms reserved to the individual. With these in place as part of the Constitution, no central government could become an instrument of tyranny. Never would the yoke of British oppression be replaced by federal oppression.

Maryland and South Carolina followed the example of Massachusetts by adding suggested amendments and then ratifying the Constitution. New Hampshire, on June 21, 1788, cast the ninth ratification necessary to put the Constitution into effect. Yet approval by Virginia and New York, because of their respective importance and geographical location, was the key to the Constitution's practical success.

Ratification in Virginia hinged on Washington. As always, he rose above factional interests. He saw the danger of having to call a second convention. As to the heated arguments against the Constitution, he found them valueless. They were, he wrote, largely "addressed to the passions of the people and obviously calculated to alarm their fears."

Modestly avoiding the center stage of public debate, Washington remained at his beloved Mount Vernon. There he worked in quiet, but effective ways to assist passage of the Constitution. In daily discussions with visitors and through written advice to influential men, he supported the Constitution and strongly advised its ratification. Finally, however, victory came on June 26, 1788, when by a close margin of 89 to 79, Virginia voted for the Constitution.

In New York, Federalists led by Hamilton won the day against strong opposition. On July 26, 1788, New York voted for ratification. Later, when North Carolina and Rhode Island approved the document, acceptance of the Constitution became unanimous by all 13 of the former British Colonies.

Putting the new Constitution and government into action was a formality. Electors of the President were chosen. Washington was the obvious and unanimous choice for President with John Adams as Vice President. By April 6, 1789, Congress was assembled, and on April 30, 1789, Washington was formally inaugurated in New York City. America, at last, had a strong federal government under a leader universally admired for his military genius, moral courage and sterling character.

Only two steps remained. The Supreme Court was organized on February 2, 1790, and the Bill of Rights was ratified on December 15, 1791. The makers of the Constitution had initially believed that it was unnecessary to forbid some of the elementary invasions of personal liberty and property rights. Many Americans, however, disagreed. They vividly remembered how the British Parliament and royal governors had trampled on these essential freedoms. Led by Massachusetts and Virginia, several states made it clear that they expected such a statement to be made part of the ratified Constitution. One of the first orders of business of the new Congress was to adopt ten articles, what we now call the Bill of Rights, as a guarantee, among other rights, of the freedoms of press, worship and assembly.

Since 1791, 16 more amendments have been added to the Constitution. Each addresses and resolves a specific issue. Each clarifies the Constitution without changing the original document's clear intention. For 200 years, the Constitution has provided a stable government even in times of deep division, civil crisis and war. In addition, it has protected the liberty of the individual. It is, in fact, the longest lasting national constitution in the world. In times when martial law and "emergency" rule are too often the norm, this is no small accomplishment.

The success of the American Constitution has inspired others. Today all but 7 of the world's 170 nations have written charters. Many, in fact, closely echo the very wording and structure of America's founding document. "All persons shall be equal before the law." "Freedom of conscience, of expression and of assembly and association." "The right to petition . . . is guaranteed." These are quotations, respectively, from the national charters of West Germany, Kenya and Costa Rica.

But simply having a constitution is not enough. It must endure and protect. In contrast to our Constitution, which has never been suspended or revoked, many constitutions around the globe last no longer than the governments that created them. A political change results in a change of constitutions. Or they are just facades of high-sounding words that only thinly disguise governments that are essentially tyrannical in nature.

In the United States, however, as Chief Justice John Marshall pointed out, the Founding Fathers created "a constitution, intended to endure for ages to come." And it has. For two centuries it has remained an anchor of liberty for America and the world. We celebrate its Bicentennial, as Americans, with great pride. And in the words of Daniel Webster, we rededicate ourselves to "one Country, one Constitution, one Destiny."

Signing of the Constitution — Christy

Chapter Two

"We the People"

A GOOD TABLE or chair stands on four sturdy legs. Similarly, the Constitution has four pillars, four basic parts, that support the overall structure. They are the Preamble, Articles, Bill of Rights and Amendments.

The word *preamble* literally means "walks before." The Preamble "walks before" and introduces the Constitution. Unlike the rest of the Constitution, it does not establish either governmental power or private right. Yet it serves two essential purposes. First, it establishes the source of the Constitution. Second, it states why the Constitution was written.

"We the People of the United States" are the source of the Constitution. It does not come from some other authority—some prince, king or even legislative body. Rather the Constitution is a direct emanation from the people themselves. It is to serve their will. The national government it creates and the individual states it discusses are servants to the people. They depend for their existence upon the permission of the people. As stated in the Declaration of Independence the people reserve the right to alter or abolish their government. The United States is to be, as Lincoln later said, a "government of the people, by the people, for the people."

Depending on the people as its source, the Constitution has as its purpose the creation of "a more perfect union" to "establish justice, insure domestic tranquility, provide for the common defense, promote the general welfare, and secure the blessing of liberty to ourselves and our posterity." These grand purposes were founded on hard realities. The Union was crumbling under the Articles of Confederation. Equal justice was lost in the jumble of conflicting state laws. Internal conflicts, like Shay's Rebellion, threatened civil chaos. Powerful European powers pressed on America's frontiers and borders. National welfare was neglected for sectional interest. Liberty itself was threatened.

Therefore, the people "do ordain and establish this Constitution for the United States of America." The "do" is crucial. As a document, the Constitution did come from the generation of 1787. As a law, however, it applies to the present generation and all generations, "our posterity," to follow. In other words, every generation recreates the Constitution. It exists in a constant state of action, of "do." By our actions and decisions, we shape this eternal document to our contemporary needs. Its broad principles are ideals, goals. We apply them to present problems. We keep the spirit of the Constitution alive and build "a more perfect union" in our time just as the Framers of the Constitution did in theirs. Each of us, "We the people," is a creator of the Constitution of our day.

Following the Preamble, the first three Articles of the Constitution establish the essential framework of the new government. The basic idea is separation and balance of power. As colonials, Americans had tasted the bitter dregs of tyranny. Just as they wanted freedom from foreign oppression, they also wanted liberty from internal domination. Government was divided into three equal parts, each with its own function: legislative, executive and judicial. Each would be exercised by a distinct body of people: Congress, the President, the Federal court system headed by the Supreme Court. No one branch of government could concentrate power. Each would balance and check the other. Barriers among the three powers and separate areas of authority would prevent excessive power in any one branch.

Article I deals with Congress. "All legislative powers" are

vested in the Senate and House of Representatives. No arm of the government except Congress can make laws. This power is not, however, a blank check. Chief Justice John Marshall, in ruling with the majority of the Supreme Court in 1819, asserted that "this government is acknowledged by all, to be one of enumerated powers." Only in specific cases where it is "necessary and proper" can Congress delegate its legislative powers, and these instances are carefully limited by the Supreme Court.

This essential point made, the rest of Article I is devoted to spelling out the actual structure of Congress, the election of Senators and Representatives, the method of creating legislation and, most important of all, the specific "enumerated" powers of Congress such as the power to levy taxes, pay national debts, regulate commerce, naturalize citizens, coin money, provide for the common defense and see to, among other things, the "general welfare" of the United States.

Article II, defining "executive power," establishes the office of the President and spells out, in just 320 words, his proper spheres of duty and authority. These include the ability to command the armed forces, provide pardons, make treaties with foreign powers, give information to Congress and "take care that the Laws be faithfully executed." Because of the President's obligation to enforce the laws made by Congress, his office has grown into one of the most important and powerful in the whole world. Yet he cannot enforce laws that do not exist. Thus Congress limits his power in that it only can pass laws. A second check on Executive authority is provided by Article III.

Article III establishes that "the judicial power of the United States shall be vested in one Supreme Court, and in such inferior courts as the Congress may from time to time ordain and establish." "Judicial power" is the ability to decide legal cases and controversies in conformity with law. This includes the Constitution as well as "standing law," such as acts of Congress, Executive orders or previous court precedents.

18

Establishing the judicial branch as an independent and co-equal department of government was in striking contrast to the lack of any judiciary under the Articles of Confederation. It was also unique in a broader sense. No other government at that time had an independent judiciary. In this one bold stroke, the Framers of the Constitution created something new under the sun. Since then, many other governments have adopted this feature, this typically American innovation in law.

Justice Story of the Supreme Court states the merits of Article III clearly: "Where there is no judicial department to interpret, pronounce, and execute the law, to decide controversies, and to enforce rights, the government must either perish of its own imbecility, or the other departments of government must usurp powers, for the purpose of commanding obedience, to the destruction of liberty. The will of those who govern will become, under such circumstances, absolute and despotic; and it is wholly immaterial whether power is vested in a single tyrant or in an assembly of tyrants."

Article III, in effect, gives the Supreme Court the ability to interpret when a law is constitutional or unconstitutional. In the latter case, it immediately becomes null and void. By committing judicial power to a separate, distinct and independent body, the Supreme Court Justices, the writers of the Constitution devised a unique way to secure the rights of life, liberty and property to every American citizen.

Article IV relates to the states. It assures that "full faith and credit" be given by each state to the public acts, records and court decisions of every other state. The states would no longer be a patchwork of conflicting laws as under the Articles of Confederation. On the contrary, a citizen's rights and immunities are preserved in all states. A fugitive in one state, for instance, cannot seek refuge in another state. Jurisdiction of the law is made uniform and harmonious in all states, and a republican form of government is guaranteed to every state in the Union. States are also protected by Article IV from invasion and domestic violence.

Article V provides for amendment to the Constitution. Two-thirds of the states, through special conventions, can propose an amendment. Approval by three-fourths of the states constitutes ratification.

Article VI is often called the "linchpin of the Constitution." Its "supremacy clause" asserts that the Constitution "shall be the supreme law of the land." All representatives of the government, federal and state, are "bound by oath or affirmation to support this constitution." They—and every citizen of America—are its guardian. Also, freedom of Religion is guaranteed by stating that "no religious test shall ever be required as a qualification to any office or public trust under the United States."

Article VII provides the process of ratification for the Constitution.

Thus in a Preamble and seven Articles, the original Constitution was complete. Or so it seemed.

Washington, as President of the Constitutional Convention and leading deputy from Virginia, was the first to sign the document. But even he had doubts. Yes, he was fully for ratification, but with the firm understanding that a Bill of Rights would be made a part of the final document. Toward this end, he supported Patrick Henry who was, in his own words, "most awfully alarmed." He considered the unamended Constitution a threat to American liberties. A clear Bill of Rights had to be attached. Others, including James Madison, agreed. On July 21, 1789, Madison persuaded the First Congress that the faith and honor of public men everywhere were pledged to amendments guaranteeing every citizen's rights and immunities. Within 2 years and 3 months, the first ten amendments, what we now call the Bill of Rights, were ratified. They so clearly complement the main body of the Constitution that today, as then, they are seen as part and parcel of the original document.

Each of the ten amendments is a specific restriction on national power. The people by inherent right had always possessed these immunities from federal interference, but passage of the Bill of Rights made this fact official and assured that the people's liberties would ever be secure against oppression by the government they themselves created.

The Bill of Rights guarantees such fundamentals as freedom of speech, press and worship; security from unreasonable search and seizure; fair trial by jury and, most importantly, the principle that any power not delegated to the federal government by the Constitution is "reserved to the States respectively, or to the people." In other words, what is not specifically restricted is left at liberty. The Bill of Rights, therefore, is a vast reservoir of freedom for all Americans. The government must prove its claim to any authority via the rights specifically enumerated to it in the Constitution. All else is left to the individual.

The final, fourth, part of the Constitution consists of the various amendments proposed and ratified since the Bill of Rights was accepted on December 15, 1791. In all they total 26. They treat such varied issues as proper election of the President, abolition of slavery, the guarantee of voting and other civil rights, creation of the income tax, definition of Senatorial tenure, the prohibition of alcoholic beverages and its repeal.

Together with the main body of the document and the Bill of Rights, these amendments fine-tune the Constitution to the needs of a changing society. The basic message of the Founding Fathers is not changed. Rather it is adapted to new understandings of what the Constitution intended and really means in the contemporary world.

On the Centennial in 1887 of the Constitutional Convention, the British statesman William Gladstone called the Constitution the most wonderful work ever struck off at a given time by the brain and purpose of man. Overstatement? Not at all. Now as we celebrate the Bicentennial of the Constitutional Convention, who can seriously disagree?

For another century the Constitution has proved its relevance and durability. It truly is our charter of liberty. In immortal words it says that man was born free and must live free. That the purpose of government is to make this possible. That rational men, abiding by laws they create for themselves and their posterity, can create a society where human dignity is cherished.

The fundamental assertion of the Constitution is faith in the integrity of the individual. Governments are, or should be, formed to protect and defend this integrity. The individual must come first. This is the essential meaning of the Constitution. This is what it said in 1787. This is what it proclaims in 1987. To be just, government must treat people as ends in themselves. The state must not be exalted over the individual. Freedom, not the survival of the state, is the true purpose of a just society and of the American Constitution.

Today America is a free nation of free individuals because generations of our fellow citizens have had the moral courage and intellectual strength to support and understand the Constitution. Many have died for their beliefs. On this Bicentennial, we inherit a unique document, a precious tradition. "We have forged," Princeton economist Robert E. Kuene points out, "an ever wider concept of freedom—it is vigorous, positive freedom, and it is not self-satisfied. The dynamism has not faltered."

Will it falter now? Will our children, grandchildren and great-grandchildren celebrate the Constitution's Tricentennial?

It is up to us.

Chapter Three

The Bill of Rights: Landmark of Liberty

YOUTH, health, ample water, clean air. We take these for granted—until they are gone. So it is with freedom. As Americans we grow up free. It is part of our nature. We give little or no thought to our daily liberties. We speak our minds, go to the church of our choice, work where we like at what we please. We enjoy freedom without even realizing we have it. Only when we encounter a recent immigrant to America do we sense in small part what it must be like to live in a closed, oppressive society where opportunities are limited or do not exist at all.

Our Founding Fathers, at least initially, were just like us today. They were fully confident of their freedoms and hardly aware that a basic articulation of them in some formal manner was necessary. After all, they had overthrown British rule. Each state controlled itself. Americans were self-evidently free.

In framing the Constitution, the idea of a statement or listing of human rights was hardly discussed. Until George Mason, almost as an afterthought, brought up the subject during the last days of the Constitutional Convention, the matter was either forgotten or ignored. James Wilson of Pennsylvania, on hearing Mason's suggestion, marveled. Such an idea "never struck the mind of any member," he remarked.

Upon reflection, however, James Madison and others saw

A More Perfect Union—*Tobey*

the merit of clearly stating "an enumeration of simple, acknowledged principles." Agreeing, the Massachusetts Constitutional Convention, in approving the Constitution, advocated adding a Bill of Rights since it "would remove the fears and quiet the apprehensions of many of the good people of this Commonwealth and more effectively guard against any undue administration of the Federal Government."

The proposed list of an American citizen's rights and immunities was to be an absolute barrier. The Declaration of Independence in Jefferson's ringing phrases had declared the "unalienable rights" of "life, liberty and the pursuit of happiness" and "that to secure these rights, governments are instituted among men." America was such a government. The Constitution had not explicitly spelled out these rights. They had to be added. The Constitution's first ten amendments are the Bill of Rights.

By making the Bill an intrinsic part of the Constitution, it is not, as some opponents asserted at the time, just a "paper check." Rather it is the irrevocable law of the land, the nation's ultimate guarantee of human dignity for every American.

The First Amendment to the Constitution (Article I of the Bill of Rights) states that Congress shall make no law abridging freedom of religion, speech, press, assembly and petition.

Before any other principle, the Bill of Rights underlines that State and Church, like oil and water, cannot mix. The world's bloody history of state-sponsored religious terrorism was already clear in the 18th century. Who could forget the infamous Spanish Inquisition or, closer to home, the persecution of several religious minorities in the colonies? Today, to the grief of people everywhere, we still see evidence of what happens when sectarian bigotry and political policy combine. Justice of the Supreme Court Hugo Black correctly pointed out that "the First Amendment has erected a wall between church and state. That wall must be kept high and impregnable.

Independence Hall—Assembly Room

We could not approve the slightest breach."

Adding to the principle of Church-State separation, Article I of the Bill of Rights states the absolute necessity of free speech and press. Only in the open exchange of all ideas can liberty grow. Today America has, by last count, 9,144 newspapers; 11,328 magazines; 9,824 radio stations; 941 commercial television stations, and 300 public television stations.

The freedoms of assembly and petition are also guaranteed by the First Amendment. Without fear of reprisal, Americans can form social groups, political parties or any other manner of mutual association and expression. We can then petition, make our wishes known, again without threat of persecution. These rights are unconditional. We meet as we please, say what we wish, and ask what we will. No article in the Bill of Rights is more profound in its significance or sweeping in its applications than Article I. It is the keystone that crowns and solidly cements the arch of all our other individual liberties. To be an American is to believe in and act by the First Amendment, first word to last.

The Second Amendment, Article II of the Bill of Rights, assures that "the right of the people to keep and bear Arms, shall not be infringed." Today sportsmen point to this article in defense of their possession of rifles and shotguns. Similarly, citizens rightfully apprehensive of their vulnerability to violence claim the right to keep firearms because of this Constitutional guarantee. On a broader scope and according to its original intention, however, the Second Amendment addresses itself to the right—and privilege—of every citizen to assure "the security of a free State." By force of arms, if necessary, liberty shall not be "infringed." Article II says in no uncertain terms that we will defend freedom at any cost.

Article III of the Bill of Rights is less contemporary in its significance. It forbids the quartering of soldiers in a citizen's home without consent of the owner during times of peace or according to the strict letter of the law during times of war. Throughout the Revolution, the British had forced colonists to house and feed "Redcoat" troops. This amendment says "Never again!"

Article IV protects "the right of the people to be secure in their persons, houses, papers and effects, against unreasonable searches and seizures." Nor can search warrants be given without "probable cause." Clearly, we all treasure the security and privacy of our homes. We often say, "A man's home is his castle." We can empathize easily with the terror of those who heard on their doors at night the pounding fist of Nazi authority. The Fourth Amendment forbids such invasions.

Yet as with all immunities, this right can be abused. Today the drug dealer is more likely to invoke the Fourth Amendment than is the average citizen. The principles of the Bill of Rights apply to *all*. Abuses, unfortunately, persist, but to dismantle the protections of the Fourth Amendment would cause more damage than good by lessening the rights of all for the sake of prosecuting a few. The integrity of this article must be preserved. Other means, difficult as they may be, must be found to check those who violate the freedom it confers.

Article V assures "due process of law" to all citizens. No person can be prosecuted twice, "double jeopardy," for the same offense, or forced to incriminate himself, or compelled to render his property to public use "without just compensation."

Article VI relates to the procedural rights of an individual once charged with a crime. The trial must be "speedy and public" before an "impartial" jury. Defendants are assured that they will be informed of "the cause of the accusation" and be able to confront witnesses in addition to being able to obtain favorable defense witnesses and the assistance of legal counsel. In other words, every citizen is guaranteed a fair trial. This amendment was written in reaction to the "Star Chamber" injustices of English common law where persons accused of felony or treason were not allowed the rights of confronting witnesses or securing counsel.

Article VII applies the concept of trial by jury to civil, as opposed to criminal, cases. Also, no civil case decided by jury shall be reexamined in any court of the United States.

Article VIII is self-explanatory: "Excessive bail shall not be required, nor excessive fines imposed, nor cruel and unusual punishments inflicted."

Article IX provides a rule of construction governing all the preceding amendments. It states that "the enumeration in the Constitution, of certain rights, shall not be construed to deny or disparage others retained by the people." The Framers of the Bill of Rights realized they could not identify *all* of a citizen's rights. Those enumerated were, at best, a partial list of the clearest, most evident human rights and immunities. Leaving additional definition to future generations, the Founding Fathers reserved for us every other possible freedom. In this sense, the Constitution is unfinished. It states goals and takes the first, though giant, steps in a long journey toward a perfect society. We are left to do our part, to carry freedom one stage farther than where we found it.

Finally, Article X makes it clear that all powers not delegated expressly by the Constitution to the federal government nor prohibited to the individual states are reserved to the states and to the people. The Founders wished to limit freedom as little as possible. Washington stated their case clearly in the letter he wrote transmitting the draft Constitution to Congress. He said:

> Individuals entering into society, must give up a share of liberty to preserve the rest. The magnitude of the sacrifice must depend as well on situation and circumstance, as on the object to be obtained. It is at all times difficult to draw with precision the line between those rights which must be surrendered, and those which may be reserved.

The great object of the Constitution and the Bill of Rights was the creation of a strong, unified nation while, at the same time, maintaining optimum freedom for all the new nation's citizens. Consequently, when a power was not absolutely necessary to the government for this purpose, it was reserved to the people.

Perhaps because we are so free, we are seldom aware of how precious liberty is. Yet we must understand and value the unique heritage we have inherited. "I have little patience," President Truman said with his typical fervor, "with those people who take the Bill of Rights for granted. The Bill of Rights, contained in the first ten amendments of the Constitution, is every American's guarantee of freedom."

We forget this truth at our peril!

> *The subject is the execution of those great powers on which the welfare of a nation essentially depends .... This provision is made in a Constitution intended to endure for ages to come and, consequently, to be adapted to the various crises of human affairs.*
>
> Chief Justice John Marshall

Our
Constitutional
Liberty

Other misfortunes may be borne, or their effects overcome. If disastrous war should sweep our commerce from the ocean, another generation may renew it; if it exhaust our treasury, future industry may replenish it; if it desolate and lay waste our fields, still, under a new cultivation they will grow green again, and ripen to future harvests. It were but a trifle if the walls of yonder capitol were to crumble, if its lofty pillars should fall, and its gorgeous decorations be all covered by the dust of the valley; all these might be rebuilt. But who shall reconstruct the fabric of demolished government? Who shall rear again the well proportioned columns of constitutional liberty? Who shall frame together the skillful architecture which unites national sovereignty with State rights, individual security, and public prosperity? No, gentlemen, if these columns fall they will be raised not again. Like the Coliseum and the Parthenon they will be destined to a mournful, a melancholy immortality. Bitterer tears, however, will flow over them than were ever shed over the monuments of Roman or Grecian art; for they will be the remnants of a more glorious edifice than Greece or Rome ever saw, the edifice of constitutional American liberty.

Daniel Webster

Chapter Four

A Nation Born of an Idea

NATIONS can be formed in many ways. Geography or climate, prince or diplomat, cultural expansion or brutal war—each has been a force by itself or in combination with others in the creation of nations. America, however, is unique. America was born of an idea. Freedom. Pilgrims seeking religious freedom came. Peasants searching for economic freedom came. Minorities yearning for cultural freedom came. Workers wanting individual freedom came.

Even before 17 million immigrants had filtered through Ellis Island in New York Harbor, America—as the "Mother of Exiles"—had offered refuge to millions more. Once here, the open lands of America's West whetted the appetite for even more liberty, and the Revolution broke forever any remaining ties to Old World ways. Americans were determined to be and remain free.

The Constitution with its Bill of Rights is the formal written statement of this resolve. Its point is simple and was squarely fixed by Justice Louis D. Brandeis. He said: "They (the makers of the Constitution) conferred, as against the Government, the right to be left alone—the most comprehensive of rights and the right most valued by civilized men."

Because of the Constitution, Americans are "let alone." Maximum freedom allows maximum results. Our individual talents are released. In "the pursuit of happiness" we can, unrestrained by needless authority, achieve our ideals to the degree that

Independence Hall

our native ability and hard work allow. By tapping and freeing the inner resources of every citizen, America has become the strongest, freest nation in the world and an example of liberty to peoples everywhere.

Shortly before his death, Thomas Jefferson penned his thoughts regarding the future of America. Our Nation's promise to mankind, he felt, was that all men someday would be free. He said: "May it [America] be to the world, what I believe it will be (to some parts sooner, to others later, but finally to all), the signal of arousing men to burst [their] chains. . . ."

The fulfillment of Jefferson's wish is still coming, but because of the Constitution and the Bill of Rights it is closer. These great documents liberate us from the oppression of excessive government while providing a stable social order in which the individual can prosper and live free. The concept is simple yet powerful. The Constitution is a social contract and the Bill of Rights its guarantee.

In the purchase of even a modest household appliance, the wise shopper looks over the guarantee—the contract made between producer and purchaser—as to just what the appliance must do under normal use. Similarly, we have warranties on our cars, contracts in our business affairs and other written agreements to cover everything from home remodeling to hospital insurance. Without such contracts we would be unprotected.

If such formal agreements are important in our everyday lives, how much more vital it is to have society based on a clear, concise contract. The Constitution is just that. It is a formal covenant between the government and the governed. Exact duties, rights and immunities are spelled out. Powers are balanced, obligations defined. Legal interpretations may affect parts of the contract. This is not entirely bad. The room provided allows for adjusting aspects of the Constitution to the changing needs of an evolving society.

As clearly, though, there are absolutes, a strong spine of principles that can never be altered. The Bill of Rights is the most obvious example. "It is my belief," Justice Hugo Black declared, "that there *are* 'absolutes' in our Bill of Rights, and that they were put there on purpose by men who knew what words meant and meant their prohibitions to be 'absolutes.'"

Imagine what life would be like without these absolute guarantees. There would be no bond of good faith between manufacturers and customers. Any claim could be made, and there would be no recourse when the shoddy purchase broke down. So with government. Without the Constitution and the Bill of Rights the citizen would be totally at the mercy of governmental whims. Nothing would limit the power of the state. Any action could be taken. Any rule could be enforced. No right or immunity would be sacred. No life secure. Minorities of any kind would be dominated by the majority of the moment. Intolerance and persecution would be the order of the day.

With no First Amendment rights, you could express nothing but the "party line." The press and all other forms of communication would be tightly censored. Only state-approved groups would be allowed to assemble. Only state-approved petitions would be allowed or considered.

With no Second Amendment, you would be forbidden the protection of bearing arms and so made defenseless before the might of the state.

Without the Third Amendment, your home, at the state's will, could be a barracks in time of peace or war.

Without the Fourth Amendment, you could be arrested without reason, your home searched, your papers and possessions plundered. The state could treat you, your loved ones and your material holdings in any way at all. You would become a helpless pawn in the play of power politics. You could call nothing your own or consider it safe since the state could take what it wants when it so desires. The individual would be nothing, the state everything.

Without the Fifth Amendment, you could be accused, tried and condemned without any legal recourse. Conditioned and brainwashed, you could be forced to testify against yourself, whatever the true facts of the case might be. The horror of Stalin's purges could be relived in American courts. Spotlighted and photographed for the public's "information," pale and harried witnesses would eagerly accuse themselves—and anyone else—of whatever "crimes" the state needed for its purpose that day. There would be no "due process of law." Accusation would be as good as guilt, and punishment would quickly follow. Nor would there be hope for your family. As a "traitor" your property could be confiscated by the government without a cent of compensation.

Without the Sixth Amendment, you would be denied the right to a speedy, public and fair trial by an impartial jury. In fact you could be accused without cause. No specific crime would have to be cited, nor could you confront your accusers or call witnesses in your defense. Deprived of legal counsel, you would have to accept the court's ruling and not even have the right of appeal. Justice would be a mockery, the court system simply a tool of the state.

Without the Seventh Amendment, no jury would be required in civil suits either, and if by chance a decision went in your favor, you could be tried again and again for the same "crime" until the state got the decision it wanted.

Without the Eighth Amendment, any bail or fine could be imposed, however excessive, and any punishment administered, no matter how cruel and unusual. As an example, during the American Revolution, English law decreed that a convicted traitor could be partially strangled and then disemboweled while still alive. For good measure, his entrails would then be burned and his body quartered. The true heroism of the "traitors" who signed America's Declaration of Independence can be better understood when one considers the fate they risked. One shudders at what punishments a 20th century state could inflict were it not hindered by such restrictions as those of the Eighth Amendment.

In sum, without the Constitution and the Bill of Rights the

government would be unlimited and uncontrolled. The individual would not be immune from any coercion. All personal freedoms would be null and void. The totalitarian state would reign supreme. Civilization as we know it would cease to exist.

This nightmare vision is, unfortunately, already a reality in some countries around the world. Freedom is rare. Lenin, ironically, agreed. He said, "It is true that liberty is precious—so precious that it must be rationed." But it need not be.

We have the American Constitution, our Nation's anchor of liberty. For two centuries it has provided us with stability, justice, prosperity and freedom. Today, guided by the Constitution, Americans continue to explore the realms of individual and social freedoms. However strong our military might and advanced our technology, America's truest and best contribution to mankind lies in the paths we have blazed on the frontiers of freedom.

We have proved via 200 years of ordered constitutional government that the state exists for the individual, not the individual for the state. We have created a nation where human dignity is cherished and the rights of minorities respected. To this we have added the highest standard of living ever experienced in the history of the world.

None of this could have been possible without our Nation's founding charters, the Constitution and the Bill of Rights. Watchwords of liberty, they have never failed us. May we never fail them.

Chapter Five

The Signers

The Signing of the Constitution—*John Froelich*

Signers of the United States Constitution
Abraham Baldwin, GA; Richard Bassett, DE; Gunning Bedford, Jr., DE; John Blair, VA; William Blount, NC; David Brearley, NJ; Jacob Broom, DE; Pierce Butler, SC; Daniel Carroll, MD; George Clymer, PA; Jonathan Dayton, NJ; John Dickinson, DE; William Few, GA; Thomas FitzSimons, PA; Benjamin Franklin, PA; Nicholas Gilman, NH; Nathaniel Gorham, MA; Alexander Hamilton, NY; Jared Ingersoll, PA; Daniel of St. Thomas Jenifer, MD; William Samuel Johnson, CT; Rufus King, MA; John Langdon, NH; William Livingston, NJ; James McHenry, MD; James Madison, VA; Thomas Mifflin, PA; Gouverneur Morris, PA; Robert Morris, PA; William Paterson, NJ; Charles Pinckney, SC; Charles Cotesworth Pinckney, SC; George Read, DE; John Rutledge, SC; Roger Sherman, CT; Richard Dobbs Spaight, Sr., NC; George Washington, VA; Hugh Williamson, NC; James Wilson, PA.

Some men look at constitutions with sanctimonious reverence, and deem them like the Ark of the Covenant, too sacred to be touched. They ascribe to the men of the preceding age a wisdom more than human, and suppose what they did to be beyond amendment.... Laws and institutions must go hand in hand with the progress of the human mind.... We might as well require a man to wear the coat that fitted him as a boy, as civilized society to remain ever under the regime of their ancestors.

Thomas Jefferson

Abraham Baldwin — Born on November 22, 1754, in North Guilford, Connecticut. Clergyman, lawyer and statesman. Chaplain in Continental Army. Member of both the Georgia Legislature and Continental Congress (1785-89). Leading Georgia delegate to Constitutional Convention where he offered a compromise on representation. United States Congressman (1789-99) and United States Senator (1799-1807). Drafted organizational plan of State educational system in Georgia. Organizer of the charter and President of University of Georgia. Died on March 4, 1807.

Richard Bassett

Richard Bassett — Born on April 2, 1745, in Cecil County, Maryland. Lawyer, statesman and jurist. Captain of a troop of Dover Light Horse in Revolution. During the years of 1776-86, was a member of the Delaware Council of Safety, the Legislature and State Constitutional Convention. Delegate to Annapolis and Federal Constitutional Conventions. United States Senator (1789-93). Chief Justice, Delaware Court of Common Pleas (1793-99). Presidential elector (1797). Governor of Delaware (1799-1801). U.S. Circuit Judge (1801). Major contributor to the First Methodist Church of Dover. Died on September 15, 1815.

Gunning Bedford, Jr. — Born in 1747 in Philadelphia, Pennsylvania. Lawyer and statesman. Member of Delaware Legislature and Council. Delegate to Continental Congress (1785-86). Delaware Attorney General (1784-89). Member of Annapolis Convention and at the Constitutional Convention a member of the Grand Committee to consider representation. Vigorous champion of States' rights. Member, Delaware Convention that ratified United States Constitution. Appointed by Washington as United States District Judge (1789-1812). Presidential elector (1789, 1793). President of the Trustees of Wilmington Academy. Died on March 30, 1812.

John Blair

John Blair — Born in 1732 in Virginia. Lawyer and jurist. Representative of the College of William and Mary to the Virginia House of Burgesses (1766-70). Member, Virginia Constitutional Convention (1776) and Privy Council (1776-78). Judge, General Court of Chancery (1778), the High Court of Chancery, and first Court of Appeals (1780). Delegate to the Constitutional Convention. Associate Justice of United States Supreme Court (1789-96). Died on August 31, 1800.

William Blount — Born on March 26, 1749 in Bertie County, North Carolina. Landowner and statesman. Paymaster to various units of North Carolina's troops during the Revolutionary War. Speaker, North Carolina Legislature. Member of Continental Congress (1782-83; 1786-87). Delegate to Constitutional Convention. Appointed by Washington as Governor and Superintendent of Indian Affairs of Territory South of Ohio River (1790). Presided over Tennessee Constitutional Convention (1796). United States Senator from Tennessee (1796). State Senator in Tennessee (1798). Died on March 21, 1800.

David Brearley.

David Brearley — Born on June 11, 1745, in Spring Grove, New Jersey. Lawyer, jurist and statesman. Lieutenant Colonel in the New Jersey Militia. Member of New Jersey Constitutional Convention. Chief Justice of New Jersey Supreme Court (1779). "Commissioner" to Constitutional Convention and member of the "grand committee." U.S. District Judge (1789-90). Vice president of the New Jersey Society of the Cincinnati and one of the compilers of an Episcopalian prayer book. Died on August 16, 1790.

Jacob Broom — Born in 1752 in Wilmington, Delaware. Surveyor, mathematician, banker and manufacturer. His maps used by Continental Army. Member of Delaware Legislature (1784-88). Chief Burgess in Wilmington (1776-85) and first Postmaster (1790-92). Delegate to Constitutional Convention. Head, Board of Directors, Bank of Delaware and founder of first cotton mill in Brandywine region (1795). Also, a member of the Board of Trustees, College of Wilmington. Died on April 25, 1810.

Pierce Butler — Born on July 11, 1744, in County Carlow, Ireland. Planter and statesman. British Army officer before Revolution. South Carolina Legislature (1778-82, 1784-89). Adjutant General of South Carolina (1779). Delegate to Continental Congress (1787) and to Constitutional Convention. United States Senator (1789-96, 1802-06). Died on February 15, 1822.

Daniel Carroll — Born on July 22, 1730, in Upper Marlboro, Maryland. Planter and statesman. Delegate to Continental Congress (1781-83) and signer of Articles of Confederation (1781). Delegate to Constitutional Convention. Commissioner for District of Columbia (1791-95) and United States Senator from Maryland (1789-91). Died on May 7, 1796.

George Clymer — Born on March 16, 1739, in Philadelphia, Pennsylvania. Merchant and banker. Captain of Volunteers and Chairman of a committee of the "Philadelphia Tea Party" (1773). Continental Treasurer (1775-76). Twice appointed special Commissioner by Washington. Member, Pennsylvania Council of Safety. Signer of Declaration of Independence. Delegate to Continental Congress (1776-77, 1780-82). Member of Pennsylvania Legislature (1785-88) and reformer of penal code. Deputy to Constitutional Convention. United States Congressman (1788-91). First president, The Bank of Philadelphia and Academy of Fine Arts. Vice president, Philadelphia Agricultural Society (1805-13). Died on January 24, 1813.

Jonathan Dayton — Born on October 16, 1760, in Elizabethtown, New Jersey. Soldier, lawyer and statesman. Officer in Continental Army and a captain at Yorktown. Member, New Jersey Assembly (1786-87, 1814-15), and Speaker, New Jersey Legislature (1790-91). Youngest delegate (age 27) to Constitutional Convention. Member of First Congress under the new United States Constitution (1788) and New Jersey Council (1789). Also, United States Congressman (1791-99) and Speaker of the House. U.S. Senator (1799-1805). Favored the Louisiana Purchase. Dayton, Ohio, named after him. Died on October 9, 1824.

John Dickinson — Born on November 8, 1732, in Talbot County, Maryland. Lawyer, statesman and educator. Speaker of the Assembly of the Lower Counties, Delaware (1760-62) and member, Pennsylvania Legislature (1762-64, 1770-76). Member of Stamp Act Congress (1765) and Continental Congress (1774-76, 1779-80). Author of *Letters from a Farmer in Pennsylvania to the Inhabitants of the British Colonies* (1767-68) and coauthor of *Declaration of the Causes of Taking up Arms to the Inhabitants of the British Colonies* (1775). Drafter and signer of the Articles of Confederation. President of the Supreme Executive Council of Delaware (1781), and of Pennsylvania. Chaired the Annapolis Convention and deputy to Constitutional Convention. Signature added to the Constitution at his request. A founder of Dickinson College (1783). Died on February 14, 1808.

William Few

William Few — Born on June 8, 1748, near Baltimore, Maryland. Lawyer, statesman, jurist and banker. Militia service in Revolution. Member of Continental Congress (1780-82, 1786-88). Delegate to Constitutional Convention. Member, Georgia Constitutional Convention, General Assembly and Executive Council. Surveyor General of Georgia and Commissioner to Indians. Judge of Second (Federal) Circuit Court (1796-99). United States Senator from Georgia (1789-93). Member of New York General Assembly (1802-05) and Inspector of State Prisons. New York City Alderman, director of Manhattan Bank (1804-14), and president of City Bank. Died on July 16, 1828.

Thomas FitzSimons — Born in 1741 in Ireland. Merchant, statesman and philanthropist. Militia officer in Revolution. Member of Pennsylvania Council of Safety and Navy Board, constructing fire ships for the Continental Navy. Member of Continental Congress, Pennsylvania Legislature and Board of Censors (1783). Deputy to Constitutional Convention. United States Congressman (1789-95). Trustee, Bank of North America, founder and president of Insurance Company of North America, president of Philadelphia Chamber of Commerce, and Trustee, University of Pennsylvania. Largest single contributor to erection of St. Augustine's Church, Philadelphia. Died on August 26, 1811.

52

Benjamin Franklin — Born January 17, 1706, in Boston, Massachusetts. Printer, scientist, statesman and diplomat. Clerk and member of Pennsylvania Assembly. Deputy Postmaster General of Philadelphia (1737-53), Deputy Postmaster General for Colonies (1753-74), and first United States Postmaster General (1775-76). Founder, American Philosophical Society, first circulating library, Philadelphia police and an academy that became the University of Pennsylvania. Delegate to Albany Congress (1754). Member of Continental Congress (1775-76). Member of committee to draft and a signer of the Declaration of Independence. Commissioner and Minister to France. Negotiator of Treaty of Paris (1783). Deputy to Constitutional Convention. Died on April 17, 1790 in Philadelphia.

Nicholas Gilman

Nicholas Gilman — Born on August 3, 1755, in Exeter, New Hampshire. Statesman. Officer in the New Hampshire Line. Investor in Continental securities. Member of Continental Congress (1786-88) and "Deputy" to Constitutional Convention. U.S. Congressman (1789-97). Appointed by Jefferson as Commissioner in Bankruptcy (1802). New Hampshire State Senator (1804-05). U.S. Senator (1805-14). Died on May 2, 1814, in Philadelphia.

Nathaniel Gorham

Nathaniel Gorham — Baptized May 21, 1738, in Charleston, Massachusetts. Statesman, judge and businessman. Member of the benevolent "Ancient" Fire Society. Delegate to Provincial Congress (1774-75). Member, Massachusetts Legislature (1781-87) and Speaker (1781-82, 1785), Massachusetts Board of War (1778-81), State Constitutional Convention (1779-80) and State Senate (1780). One of the incorporators of Charles River Bridge (1785). Judge of Middlesex Court of Common Pleas (1785). Member of Continental Congress (1782, 1783, 1785-87), elected President of Congress June 6, 1786. Delegate to Constitutional Convention and Chairman of Committee of the Whole, May 30, 1787. Died on June 11, 1796.

Alexander Hamilton — Born on January 11, 1757 in Nevis, British West Indies. Soldier, lawyer and civil servant. Lieutenant colonel in Continental Army. Secretary and aide-de-camp to Washington. Was a commander of troops under LaFayette at Yorktown (1781). Member of Continental Congress (1782-83; 1788). At the Annapolis Convention (1786) drafted a report that led to the Constitutional Convention. Delegate to Convention and part author of *The Federalist* (1787-88). First Secretary of the Treasury (1789-95). Inspector General, U.S. Provisional Army (1798-1800). Financial genius and major architect of American government. Died on July 12, 1804.

Jared Ingersoll

Jared Ingersoll — Born on October 27, 1749, in New Haven, Connecticut. Lawyer and jurist. Member of Continental Congress (1780-81). Delegate to Constitutional Convention. Attorney General of Pennsylvania (1790-99, 1811-17). United States District Attorney General for Pennsylvania (1800-01). Philadelphia City Solicitor (1798-1801), and advocate before U.S. Supreme Court. Member of Philadelphia Common Council (1789). Candidate for U.S. Vice President (1812). Presiding judge for city and county of Philadelphia (1821-22). Died on October 31, 1822.

Daniel of St. Thomas Jenifer — Born in 1723 near Port Tobacco, Maryland. Planter and statesman. Agent and Receiver-General for two Lords Proprietary of Maryland. Justice of the Peace and a member of the Pennsylvania-Delaware Boundary Commission. Member of Provincial Court (1766) and Governor's Council (1773-76). President, Maryland Council of Safety (1776-77) and Maryland Senate (1777-80). Delegate to Continental Congress (1779-82). Intendent of Maryland Revenues and Commissioner representing Maryland at the Alexandria-Mount Vernon Conference (1785). Delegate to Constitutional Convention. He was a close friend of Washington. Died on November 16, 1790.

William Samuel Johnson — Born on October 7, 1727, in Stratford, Connecticut. Statesman and jurist. Member, Connecticut Legislator (1761-76) and Governor's Council. Delegate to Stamp Act Congress (1765) and drafter of "Address to the King." Colonial agent in England (1767-71). Judge of Connecticut Superior Court (1772). Officer, Connecticut Militia. Elected to Continental Congress (1774) but declined service. Delegate to Confederation Congress (1784-87) and Constitutional Convention. Served as Chairman of the Committee on Style. United States Senator (1789-91). President of Columbia College (1787-1800). Died on November 14, 1819.

ſ King

Rufus King — Born on March 24, 1755, in Scarboro, Maine. Lawyer, statesman and diplomat. Military service in Revolution. Member, Massachusetts General Court (1783-85). Delegate to Continental Congress (1784-86) and Chairman of Committee on Finance (1786). A drafter of the Ordinance of 1787. Delegate to and most eloquent orator at Constitutional Convention. Member of Constitutional Committee on Style and Arrangement. Twice New York Assemblyman. United States Senator (1789-1801; 1813-25). Director of Bank of United States (1791). United States Minister Plenipotentiary to Great Britain (1796-1803; 1825-26). Candidate for President of the United States (1816) and twice for Vice President (1804 and 1808). Author of Navigation Act of 1818. Died on April 29, 1827.

John Langdon

John Langdon — Born on June 26, 1741, in Portsmouth, New Hampshire. Soldier, merchant and statesman. Revolutionary militia leader at Saratoga and in Rhode Island campaign. Shipbuilder for the Continental Congress. Speaker (1775, 1786-87) and member of the New Hampshire Legislature (1777-81, 1801-05). Agent of Continental Navy (1776). Financier of General Stark's expedition against General Burgoyne (1777). Twice President of New Hampshire (1785-86, 1788-89). Delegate to Federal Constitutional Convention and pivotal leader of ratification in New Hampshire. First Presiding Officer, U.S. Senate (1789) and U.S. Senator (1789-1801). Governor of New Hampshire (1805-08, 1810-12). Died on September 18, 1819.

William Livingston — Born in November 1723, in Albany, New York. Lawyer, scholar and statesman. Member of New York Legislature and Essex County New Jersey Committee of Correspondence. Delegate to Continental Congress (1774-76). Author of *Philosophic Solitude.* A commander of New Jersey Revolutionary Militia (1776). First Governor of New Jersey. Delegate to the Constitutional Convention. Died on July 25, 1790.

James McHenry (signature)

James McHenry — Born on November 16, 1753, in Ballymena, County Antrim, Ireland. Physician and soldier. Surgeon in Continental Army, and Senior Surgeon at Valley Forge. Military secretary to Washington (1778-80) and Aide to LaFayette (1780). Member Maryland Senate (1781-86; 1791-96). Member of Continental Congress (1783-86). Delegate to Constitutional Convention. His personal journal of the proceedings of the Convention is regarded as one of the most valuable resources for historians. United States Secretary of War (1796-1800). Baltimore's Fort McHenry, site of the composition of "The Star-Spangled Banner" in 1814 by Francis Scott Key, named after him. Died on May 3, 1816.

James Madison Jr.

James Madison — Born on March 16, 1751, in Port Conway, Virginia. Lawyer and Statesman. Committee of Public Safety of Orange County (1775). Member of committee to draft the state Constitution at Virginia Convention (1776). Member of Virginia Assembly (1778-79), House of Delegates (1776-77; 1784-86), and Governor's Council (1778). Delegate to Continental Congress (1780-83; 1787-88). Member of Annapolis Convention (1786). At the Constitutional Convention (1787) was the chief recorder of the proceedings. Authorship of a number of the *Federalist Papers* may be credited to Madison. Proposed first ten amendments (the Bill of Rights) to United States Constitution. United States Congressman (1789-97). Secretary of State (1801-09). Fourth President of the United States (1809), reelected (1812). Rector, University of Virginia (1826-36). Died on June 28, 1836.

Thomas Mifflin — Born on January 10, 1744, in Philadelphia, Pennsylvania. Merchant and statesman. Member, Pennsylvania Provincial Assembly and Pennsylvania Legislature. Member of Continental Congress (1774-75, 1782-84) and its President (1783-84). Aide to Washington. Member, Board of War. Major general and Quartermaster-General, Continental Army. Chairman of Pennsylvania Constitutional Convention (1788-90) and delegate to Federal Constitutional Convention (1787). Governor of Pennsylvania (1790-99). Died on January 20, 1800.

Gouverneur Morris — Born on January 31, 1752, in Morrisania, New York. Lawyer, statesman and diplomat. Member, New York Provincial Congress (1775-77), New York State Constitutional Convention and Council of Safety. Chairman of several leading committees and diplomatic assignments in Continental Congress (1778-79). Author of *Observations on the American Revolution* (1779). Signer, Articles of Confederation. Assistant Superintendent of Finance (1781-85). Drew up plan for decimal system of coinage and invented the word "cent." Deputy from Pennsylvania to Constitutional Convention. Minister to France (1792-94). U.S. Senator from New York (1800-03). Supporter of Louisiana Purchase. Chairman, Erie Canal Commission. Died on November 6, 1816.

Robert Morris — Born on January 31, 1734, in Liverpool, England. Merchant and banker. Served on Pennsylvania Committee of Correspondence and Council of Safety (1775-76). Member, Pennsylvania Legislature and Continental Congress (1775-78). Signer of Declaration of Independence and Articles of Confederation. Superintendent of Finance (1782-84). Founder, Bank of North America (1781). Delegate to Annapolis Convention (1786) and Constitutional Convention (1787). United States Senator (1789-95). Died on May 8, 1806 in Philadelphia.

William Paterson — Born on December 24, 1745, in County Antrim, Ireland. Lawyer and statesman. The College of New Jersey graduate in 1763, M.A. in 1766 delivering oration on "Patriotism." Founder, "Well-Meaning Society" (1765-68). Member, New Jersey Provincial Congress (1755), Constitutional Convention (New Jersey, 1776), and Council of Safety (1776-77). Officer of battalion of minutemen (1777). First New Jersey Attorney General (1776-83). Commissioner to Federal Constitutional Convention and advocate of small States' rights. United States Senator (1789-90). An author of the *Laws of the State of New Jersey* (1800). Governor and Chancellor of New Jersey (1791-93). Associate Justice, United States Supreme Court (1793-1806). Died on September 9, 1806, in Albany, New York.

Charles Pinckney

Charles Pinckney — Born on October 26, 1757, in Charleston, South Carolina. Lawyer, statesman and diplomat. Lieutenant of the Charleston Regiment of Militia during the Revolution. Member of South Carolina Legislature and Council (1779-80; 1786-89; 1806; 1810-14). Delegate to Continental Congress (1777-78; 1784-87) and Delegate to Constitutional Convention. Governor of South Carolina (1789-92; 1796-98; 1806-08), and President of State Constitutional Convention (1790). United States Senator (1799-1801) and Minister to Spain (1801-05). United States Congressman (1819-21). Died on October 29, 1824.

Charles Cotesworth Pinckney

Charles Cotesworth Pinckney — Born on February 25, 1746, in Charleston, South Carolina. Lawyer, soldier, diplomat and statesman. Member, South Carolina Assembly (1769), Acting Attorney General (1773), Provincial Congress (1775), and Council of Safety (1776). Colonel in Continental Army and Aide to General Washington. Member, South Carolina lower House (1778,1782), and President of South Carolina Senate (1779). Delegate to Constitutional Convention. Minister to France (1796). Major general in the United States Provisional Army (1798). Candidate for Vice President (1800), and for President (1804 and 1808). Was first elected member of the Board of Trustees, South Carolina College (now University of South Carolina). Died on August 16, 1825.

George Read — Born on September 18, 1733, near North East, Cecil County, Maryland. Lawyer and jurist. Delaware Provincial Assembly (1765-77). Delaware Legislature Council (1776-79, 1782-88). Attorney General for the Lower Counties of Delaware (1763-74) and member of Continental Congress (1774-77). Signer of Declaration of Independence. Presiding officer, Delaware Constitutional Convention (1776) and President of Delaware (1777-78). Judge, Court of Appeals in admiralty cases (1782). Delegate to Annapolis Convention (1786). Deputy to Constitutional Convention. Led Delaware to be the first State to ratify the Constitution on December 7, 1789. United States Senator (1789-93). Chief Justice of Delaware (1793-98). Died on September 21, 1798.

John Rutledge — Born in September 1739, in Charleston, South Carolina. Lawyer, statesman and jurist. Member of South Carolina Provincial Assembly (1761-74). Attorney General of South Carolina (1764-65). Member, South Carolina Legislature (1774-78; 1784-90) and Council of Safety (1776). Delegate to Stamp Act Congress (1765) and Continental Congress (1774-75; 1782-83). Member of South Carolina Constitutional Convention. President of lower house of Legislature (1776-78) and Governor of South Carolina (1779-82). Delegate to Constitutional Convention. Judge of Chancery Court (1784) and Associate Justice of U.S. Supreme Court (1789-91). Chief Justice of South Carolina Supreme Court (1791) and nominated for Chief Justice of the United States Supreme Court (1795). Died on July 18, 1800.

Roger Sherman

Roger Sherman — Born on April 19, 1721, in Newton, Massachusetts. Cobbler, almanac maker, jurist and statesman. Surveyor of New Haven County (1745-58). Member of Connecticut Legislature (1755, 1758-61), and Council of Safety. Justice of County Court (1759). Member of committee appointed to draft the Declaration of Independence, which he later signed. Judge of Superior Court of Connecticut (1766-89). Member of Continental Congress (1774-81, 1783-84). Member of committee appointed to draft the Articles of Confederation which he later signed. Member of Constitutional Convention. Mayor of New Haven, Connecticut, and treasurer of Yale College. United States Congressman (1789-91) and United States Senator (1791-93). Died on July 23, 1793.

Richard Dobbs Spaight, Sr. — Born on March 25, 1758, in New Bern, North Carolina. Statesman. Officer in Revolutionary Militia. Member of North Carolina Legislature (1779; 1781-83; 1785-87; 1792). Delegate to Continental Congress (1783-85) and Delegate to Constitutional Convention. Three-term Governor of North Carolina, first elected in 1792. Presidential Elector (1793). United States Congressman (1798-1801) and North Carolina State Senator (1801; 1802). Died on September 6, 1802.

George Washington — Born on February 22, 1732, in Virginia. Frontier surveyor. Lieutenant colonel during French and Indian War. Commander of the Virginia Militia. Member of the Virginia House of Burgesses, 1759-74. Delegate to the First and Second Continental Congresses. Commander in Chief of the Continental Army. President of the Constitutional Convention. First President of the United States, 1789, and reelected in 1793. Died on December 14, 1799.

Hugh Williamson — Born on December 5, 1735, in West Nottingham, Pennsylvania. Merchant, physician and scholar. Professor of mathematics, College of Philadelphia (1760-63). Shared experiments with Franklin. Elected to American Philosophical Society (1768). Surgeon General of North Carolina Militia during Revolution. Member of North Carolina Legislature (1782; 1785). Delegate to Continental Congress (1782-85; 1787-89). Delegate to Constitutional Convention. United States Congressman (1789-93). One of the original trustees, University of North Carolina; also a trustee, College of Physicians and Surgeons; and trustee, University of State of New York. Author of numerous scientific studies. Died on May 22, 1819.

James Wilson

James Wilson — Born on September 14, 1742, in Carsker-
do, near St. Andrews, Scotland. Lawyer and jurist. Head of
Pennsylvania Committee of Correspondence (1774), and
member, Pennsylvania Provincial Conference (1775). Signer
of Declaration of Independence. Delegate to First Continental Congress (1774), also served terms in Congress (1775-77,
1785-87). Member, Continental Board of War (1776-77). Advocate General for France in America (1779-83). Deputy to Constitutional Convention. Professor of Law at the College of Pennsylvania (1789). Associate Justice of United States Supreme
Court (1789-98). Drafter of Pennsylvania Constitution (1790).
Defender of national authority in *Chisholm* v. *Georgia* (1793).
Died on August 21, 1798.

Scene at the Signing of the Constitution—*Christy*

> *The Constitution of the United States was made not merely for the generation that then existed, but for posterity—unlimited, undefined, endless perpetual posterity.*
>
> Henry Clay

Chapter Six

The Constitution of the United States

The following official copy of the United States Constitution has been prepared and supplied by the Commission on the Bicentennial of the United States Constitution.

Preamble

We the People of the United States, in Order to form a more perfect Union, establish Justice, insure domestic Tranquility, provide for the common defence, promote the general Welfare, and secure the Blessings of Liberty to ourselves and our Posterity, do ordain and establish this Constitution for the United States of America.

Article. I.

Section. 1. All legislative Powers herein granted shall be vested in a Congress of the United States, which shall consist of a Senate and House of Representatives.

Section. 2. The House of Representatives shall be composed of Members chosen every second Year by the People of the several States, and the Electors in each State shall have the Qualifications requisite for Electors of the most numerous Branch of the State Legislature.

No Person shall be a Representative who shall not have attained to the Age of twenty five Years, and been seven Years a Citizen of the United States, and who shall not, when elected, be an Inhabitant of that State in which he shall be chosen.

[Representatives and [direct Taxes] shall be apportioned among the several States [which may be included within this Union,] according to their respective Numbers, which shall be determined by adding to the whole Number of free Persons, including those bound to Service for a Term of Years, and excluding Indians not taxed, three fifths of all other Persons.]* The actual Enumeration shall be made within three Years after the first Meeting of the Congress of the United States, and within every subsequent Term of ten Years, in such Manner

---

*Changed by section 2 of the Fourteenth Amendment.

as they shall by Law direct. The number of Representatives shall not exceed one for every thirty Thousand, but each State shall have at Least one Representative; and until such enumeration shall be made, the State of New Hampshire shall be entitled to chuse three, Massachusetts eight, Rhode-Island and Providence Plantations one, Connecticut five, New-York six, New Jersey four, Pennsylvania eight, Delaware one, Maryland six, Virginia ten, North Carolina five, South Carolina five, and Georgia three.

When vacancies happen in the Representation from any State, the Executive Authority thereof shall issue Writs of Election to fill such Vacancies.

The House of Respresentatives shall chuse their Speaker and other Officers; and shall have the sole Power of Impeachment.

Section. 3. The Senate of the United States shall be composed of two Senators from each State, [chosen by the Legislature thereof,]* for six Years; and each Senator shall have one Vote.

Immediately after they shall be assembled in Consequence of the first Election, they shall be divided as equally as may be into three Classes. The Seats of the Senators of the first Class shall be vacated at the Expiration of the second Year, of the second Class at the Expiration of the fourth Year, and of the third Class at the Expiration of the sixth Year, so that one third may be chosen every second Year; [and if Vacancies happen by Resignation, or otherwise, during the Recess of the Legislature of any State, the Executive thereof may make temporary Appointments until the next Meeting of the Legislature, which shall then fill such Vacancies.]**

No Person shall be a Senator who shall not have attained to the Age of thirty Years, and been nine Years a Citizen of

---

*Changed by section 1 of the Seventeenth Amendment.
**Changed by section 2 of the Seventeenth Amendment.

the United States, and who shall not, when elected, be an Inhabitant of that State for which he shall be chosen.

The Vice President of the United States shall be President of the Senate, but shall have no Vote, unless they be equally divided.

The Senate shall chuse their other Officers, and also a President pro tempore, in the Absence of the Vice President, or when he shall exercise the Office of President of the United States.

The Senate shall have the sole Power to try all Impeachments. When sitting for that Purpose, they shall be on Oath or Affirmation. When the President of the United States is tried, the Chief Justice shall preside: And no Person shall be convicted without the Concurrence of two thirds of the Members present.

Judgment in Cases of Impeachment shall not extend further than to removal from Office, and disqualification to hold and enjoy any Office of honor, Trust or Profit under the United States: but the Party convicted shall nevertheless be liable and subject to Indictment, Trial, Judgment and Punishment, according to Law.

Section. 4. The Times, Places and Manner of holding Elections for Senators and Representatives, shall be prescribed in each State by the Legislature thereof; but the Congress may at any time by Law make or alter such Regulations, except as to the Places of chusing Senators.

The Congress shall assemble at least once in every Year, and such Meeting shall be [on the first Monday in December,]* unless they shall by Law appoint a different Day.

Section. 5. Each House shall be the Judge of the Elections, Returns and Qualifications of its own Members, and a

---

*Changed by section 2 of the Twentieth Amendment.

Majority of each shall constitute a Quorum to do Business; but a smaller Number may adjourn from day to day, and may be authorized to compel the Attendance of absent Members, in such Manner, and under such Penalties as each House may provide.

Each House may determine the Rules of its Proceedings, punish its Members for disorderly Behaviour, and, with the Concurrence of two thirds, expel a Member.

Each House shall keep a Journal of its Proceedings, and from time to time publish the same, excepting such Parts as may in their Judgment require Secrecy; and the Yeas and Nays of the Members of either House on any question shall, at the Desire of one fifth of those Present, be entered on the Journal.

Neither House, during the Session of Congress, shall, without the Consent of the other, adjourn for more than three days, nor to any other Place than that in which the two Houses shall be sitting.

Section. 6. The Senators and Representatives shall receive a Compensation for their Services, to be ascertained by Law, and paid out of the Treasury of the United States. They shall in all Cases, except Treason, Felony and Breach of the Peace, be privileged from Arrest during their Attendance at the Session of their respective Houses, and in going to and returning from the same; and for any Speech or Debate in either House, they shall not be questioned in any other Place.

No Senator or Representative shall, during the Time for which he was elected, be appointed to any civil Office under the Authority of the United States, which shall have been created, or the Emoluments whereof shall have been encreased during such time; and no Person holding any Office under the United States, shall be a Member of either House during his Continuance in Office.

Section. 7. All Bills for raising Revenue shall originate in the House of Representatives; but the Senate may propose or concur with Amendments as on other Bills.

Every Bill which shall have passed the House of Representatives and the Senate, shall, before it becomes a Law, be presented to the President of the United States; If he approves he shall sign it, but if not he shall return it, with his Objections to that House in which it shall have originated, who shall enter the Objections at large on their Journal, and proceed to reconsider it. If after such Reconsideration two thirds of that House shall agree to pass the Bill, it shall be sent, together with the Objections, to the other House, by which it shall likewise be reconsidered, and if approved by two thirds of that House, it shall become a Law. But in all such Cases the Votes of both Houses shall be determined by yeas and Nays, and the Names of the Persons voting for and against the Bill shall be entered on the Journal of each House respectively. If any Bill shall not be returned by the President within ten Days (Sundays excepted) after it shall have been presented to him, the Same shall be a Law, in like Manner as if he had signed it, unless the Congress by their Adjournment prevent its Return, in which Case it shall not be a Law.

Every Order, Resolution, or Vote to which the Concurrence of the Senate and House of Representatives may be necessary (except on a question of Adjournment) shall be presented to the President of the United States; and before the Same shall take Effect, shall be approved by him, or being disapproved by him, shall be repassed by two thirds of the Senate and House of Representatives, according to the Rules and Limitations prescribed in the Case of a Bill.

Section. 8. The Congress shall have Power to lay and collect Taxes, Duties, Imposts and Excises, to pay the Debts and provide for the common Defence and general Welfare of the United States; but all Duties, Imposts and Excises shall be uniform throughout the United States.

To borrow Money on the credit of the United States;

To regulate Commerce with foreign Nations, and among the

several States, and with the Indian Tribes;

To establish a uniform Rule of Naturalization, and uniform Laws on the subject of Bankruptcies throughout the United States;

To coin Money, regulate the Value thereof, and of foreign Coin, and fix the Standard of Weights and Measures;

To provide for the Punishment of counterfeiting the Securities and current Coin of the United States;

To establish Post Offices and post Roads;

To promote the Progress of Science and useful Arts, by securing for limited Times to Authors and Inventors the exclusive Right to their respective Writings and Discoveries;

To constitute Tribunals inferior to the supreme Court;

To define and punish Piracies and Felonies committed on the high Seas, and Offenses against the Law of Nations;

To declare War, grant Letters of Marque and Reprisal, and make Rules concerning Captures on Land and Water;

To raise and support Armies, but no Appropriation of Money to that Use shall be for a longer Term than two Years;

To provide and maintain a Navy;

To make Rules for the Government and Regulation of the land and naval Forces;

To provide for calling forth the Militia to execute the Laws of the Union, suppress Insurrections and repel Invasions;

To provide for organizing, arming, and disciplining, the Militia, and for governing such Part of them as may be employed in the Service of the United States, reserving to the States respectively, the Appointment of the Officers, and the Authority of training the Militia according to the discipline prescribed by Congress;

To exercise exclusive Legislation in all Cases whatsoever, over such District (not exceeding ten Miles square) as may, by Cession of particular States, and the Acceptance of Congress, become the Seat of the Government of the United States, and to exercise like Authority over all Places purchased by the Consent of the Legislature of the State in which the Same shall be, for the Erection of Forts, Magazines, Arsenals, dock-Yards and other needful Buildings;—And

To make all Laws which shall be necessary and proper for carrying into Execution the foregoing Powers, and all other Powers vested by this Constitution in the Government of the United States, or in any Department or Officer thereof.

Section. 9. The Migration or Importation of such Persons as any of the States now existing shall think proper to admit, shall not be prohibited by the Congress prior to the Year one thousand eight hundred and eight, but a Tax or duty may be imposed on such Importation, not exceeding ten dollars for each Person.

The Privilege of the Writ of Habeas Corpus shall not be suspended, unless when in Cases of Rebellion or Invasion the public Safety may require it.

No Bill of Attainder or ex post facto Law shall be passed.

[No Capitation, or other direct, Tax shall be laid, unless in Proportion to the Census or Enumeration herein before directed to be taken.]*

No Tax or Duty shall be laid on Articles exported from any State.

No Preference shall be given by any Regulation of Commerce or Revenue to the Ports of one State over those of another: nor shall Vessels bound to, or from, one State, be obliged to enter, clear, or pay Duties in another.

No Money shall be drawn from the Treasury, but in Consequence of Appropriations made by Law; and a regular Statement and Account of the Receipts and Expenditures of all public Money shall be published from time to time.

No Title of Nobility shall be granted by the United States: And no Person holding any Office of Profit or Trust under them, shall, without the Consent of the Congress, accept of any present, Emolument, Office, or Title, of any kind whatever, from any King, Prince, or foreign State.

---

*Changed by the Sixteenth Amendment.

Section. 10. No State shall enter into any Treaty, Alliance, or Confederation; grant Letters of Marque and Reprisal; coin Money; emit Bills of Credit; make any Thing but gold and silver Coin a Tender in Payment of Debts; pass any Bill of Attainder, ex post facto Law, or Law impairing the Obligation of Contracts, or grant any Title of Nobility.

No State shall, without the Consent of the Congress, lay any Imposts or Duties on Imports or Exports, except what may be absolutely necessary for executing its inspection Laws: and the net Produce of all Duties and Imposts, laid by any State on Imports or Exports, shall be for the Use of the Treasury of the United States; and all such Laws shall be subject to the Revision and Controul of the Congress.

No State shall, without the Consent of Congress, lay any Duty of Tonnage, keep Troops, or Ships of War in time of Peace, enter into any Agreement or Compact with another State, or with a foreign Power, or engage in War, unless actually invaded, or in such imminent Danger as will not admit of delay.

Article. II.

Section. 1. The executive Power shall be vested in a President of the United States of America. He shall hold his Office during the Term of four Years, and, together with the Vice President, chosen for the same Term, be elected, as follows.

Each State shall appoint, in such Manner as the Legislature thereof may direct, a Number of Electors, equal to the whole Number of Senators and Representatives to which the State may be entitled in the Congress: but no Senator or Representative, or Person holding an Office of Trust or Profit under the United States, shall be appointed an Elector.

[The Electors shall meet in their respective States, and vote by Ballot for two Persons, of whom one at least shall not be an Inhabitant of the same State with themselves. And they shall make a List of all the Persons voted for, and of the Number of Votes for each; which List they shall sign and certify, and transmit sealed to the Seat of the Government of the United States, directed to the President of the Senate. The President of the Senate shall, in the Presence of the Senate and House of Representatives, open all the Certificates, and the Votes shall then be counted. The Person having the greatest Number of Votes shall be the President, if such Number be a Majority of the whole Number of Electors appointed; and if there be more than one who have such Majority, and have an equal Number of Votes, then the House of Representatives shall immediately chuse by Ballot one of them for President; and if no Person have a Majority, then from the five highest on the List the said House shall in like Manner chuse the President. But in chusing the President, the Votes shall be taken by States, the Representation from each State having one Vote; A quorum for this Purpose shall consist of a Member or Members from two thirds of the States, and a Majority of all the States shall be necessary to a Choice. In every Case, after the Choice of the President, the Person having the greatest Number of Votes of the Electors shall be the Vice President. But if there should remain two or more who have equal Votes, the Senate shall chuse from them by Ballot the Vice President.]*

The Congress may determine the Time of chusing the Electors, and the Day on which they shall give their Votes; which Day shall be the same throughout the United States.

No Person except a natural born Citizen, or a Citizen of the United States, at the time of the Adoption of this Constitution, shall be eligible to the Office of the President; neither shall any person be eligible to that Office who shall not have attained to the Age of thirty five Years, and been fourteen Years a Resident within the United States.

[In Case of the Removal of the President from Office, or of his Death, Resignation, or Inability to discharge the Powers and Duties of the said Office, the Same shall devolve on the

---

*Changed by the Twelfth Amendment.

Vice President, and the Congress may by Law provide for the Case of Removal, Death, Resignation or Inability, both of the President and Vice President, declaring what Officer shall then act as President, and such Officer shall act accordingly, until the Disability be removed, or a President shall be elected.]*

The President shall, at stated Times, receive for his Services, a Compensation, which shall neither be increased nor diminished during the Period for which he shall have been elected, and he shall not receive within that Period any other Emolument from the United States, or any of them.

Before he enter on the Execution of his Office, he shall take the following Oath or Affirmation:—"I do solemnly swear (or affirm) that I will faithfully execute the Office of President of the United States, and will to the best of my Ability, preserve, protect and defend the Constitution of the United States."

Section. 2. The President shall be Commander in Chief of the Army and Navy of the United States, and of the Militia of the several States, when called into the actual Service of the United States; he may require the Opinion, in writing, of the principal Officer in each of the executive Departments, upon any Subject relating to the Duties of their respective Offices, and he shall have Power to grant Reprieves and Pardons for Offenses against the United States, except in Cases of Impeachment.

He shall have Power, by and with the Advice and Consent of the Senate, to make Treaties, provided two thirds of the Senators present concur; and he shall nominate, and by and with the Advice and Consent of the Senate, shall appoint Ambassadors, other public Ministers and Consuls, Judges of the supreme Court, and all other Officers of the United States, whose Appointments are not herein otherwise provided for, and which shall be established by Law: but the Congress may

---

*Changed by the Twenty-Fifth Amendment.

by Law vest the Appointment of such inferior Officers, as they think proper, in the President alone, in the Courts of Law, or in the Heads of Departments.

The President shall have Power to fill up all Vacancies that may happen during the Recess of the Senate, by granting Commissions which shall expire at the End of their next Session.

Section. 3. He shall from time to time give to the Congress Information of the State of the Union, and recommend to their Consideration such Measures as he shall judge necessary and expedient; he may, on extraordinary Occasions, convene both Houses, or either of them, with and in Case of Disagreement between them, with Respect to the Time of Adjournment, he may adjourn them to such Time as he shall think proper; he shall receive Ambassadors and other public Ministers; he shall take Care that the Laws be faithfully executed, and shall Commission all the Officers of the United States.

Section. 4. The President, Vice President, and all civil Officers of the United States, shall be removed from Office on Impeachment for, and Conviction of, Treason, Bribery, or other high Crimes and Misdemeanors.

Article. III.

Section. 1. The judicial Power of the United States, shall be vested in one supreme Court, and in such inferior Courts as the Congress may from time to time ordain and establish. The Judges, both of the supreme and inferior Courts, shall hold their Offices during good Behaviour, and shall, at stated Times, receive for their Services, a Compensation, which shall not be diminished during their Continuance in Office.

Section. 2. The judicial Power shall extend to all Cases, in Law and Equity, arising under this Constitution, the Laws of the United States, and Treaties made, or which shall be made, under their Authority;—to all Cases affecting Ambassadors, other public Ministers and Consuls;—to all Cases of admiralty and maritime Jurisdiction;—to Controversies to which the United States shall be a Party;—to Controversies between two or more States; [between a State and Citizens of another state;—]* between Citizens of different States—between Citizens of the same State claiming Lands under Grants of different States, and [between a State, or the Citizens thereof, and foreign States, Citizens or Subjects.]*

In all Cases affecting Ambassadors, other public Ministers and Consuls, and those in which a State shall be Party, the supreme Court shall have original Jurisdiction. In all the other Cases before mentioned, the supreme Court shall have appellate Jurisdiction, both as to Law and Fact, with such Exceptions, and under such Regulations as the Congress shall make.

The Trial of all Crimes, except in Cases of Impeachment; shall be by Jury; and such Trial shall be held in the State where the said Crimes shall have been committed; but when not committed within any State, the Trial shall be at such Place or Places as the Congress may by Law have directed.

Section. 3. Treason against the United States, shall consist only in levying War against them, or in adhering to their Enemies, giving them Aid and Comfort. No Person shall be convicted of Treason unless on the Testimony of two Witnesses to the same overt Act, or on Confession in open Court.

The Congress shall have Power to declare the Punishment of Treason, but no Attainder of Treason shall work Corruption of Blood, or Forfeiture except during the Life of the Person attainted.

Article. IV.

Section. 1. Full Faith and Credit shall be given in each State to the public Acts, Records, and judicial Proceedings of

---

*Changed by the Eleventh Amendment.

every other State; And the Congress may by general Laws prescribe the Manner in which such Acts, Records and Proceedings shall be proved, and the Effect thereof.

Section. 2. The Citizens of each State shall be entitled to all Privileges and Immunities of Citizens in the several States.

A Person charged in any State with Treason, Felony, or other Crime, who shall flee from Justice, and be found in another State, shall on Demand of the executive Authority of the State from which he fled, be delivered up, to be removed to the State having Jurisdiction of the Crime.

[No Person held to Service or Labour in one State, under the Laws thereof, escaping into another, shall, in Consequence of any Law or Regulation therein, be discharged from such Service or Labour, but shall be delivered up on Claim of the Party to whom such Service or Labour may be due.]*

Section. 3. New States may be admitted by the Congress into this Union; but no new State shall be formed or erected within the Jurisdiction of any other State; nor any State be formed by the Junction of two or more States, or Parts of States, without the Consent of the Legislatures of the States concerned as well as of the Congress.

The Congress shall have Power to dispose of and make all needful Rules and Regulations respecting the Territory or other Property belonging to the United States; and nothing in this Constitution shall be so construed as to Prejudice any Claims of the United States, or of any particular State.

Section. 4. The United States shall guarantee to every State in this Union a Republican Form of Government, and shall protect each of them against Invasion; and on Application of the Legislature, or of the Executive (when the Legislature cannot be convened) against domestic Violence.

---

*Changed by the Thirteenth Amendment.

Article. V.

The Congress, whenever two thirds of both Houses shall deem it necessary, shall propose Amendments to this Constitution, or, on the Application of the Legislatures of two thirds of the several States, shall call a Convention for proposing Amendments, which, in either Case, shall be valid to all Intents and Purposes, as Part of this Constitution, when ratified by the Legislatures of three fourths of the several States, or by Conventions in three fourths thereof, as the one or the other Mode of Ratification may be proposed by the Congress; Provided that no Amendment which may be made prior to the Year One thousand eight hundred and eight shall in any Manner affect the first and fourth Clauses in the Ninth Section of the first Article; and that no State, without its Consent, shall be deprived of its equal Suffrage in the Senate.

Article. VI.

All Debts contracted and Engagements entered into, before the Adoption of this Constitution, shall be as valid against the United States under this Constitution, as under the Confederation.

This Constitution, and the Laws of the United States which shall be made in Pursuance thereof; and all Treaties made, or which shall be made, under the Authority of the United States, shall be the supreme Law of the Land; and the Judges in every State shall be bound thereby, any Thing in the Constitution or Laws of any State to the Contrary notwithstanding.

The Senators and Representatives before mentioned, and the Members of the several State Legislatures, and all executive and judicial Officers, both of the United States and of the several States, shall be bound by Oath or Affirmation, to support this Constitution; but no religious Test shall ever be required as a Qualification to any Office or public Trust under the United States.

Article. VII.

The Ratification of the Conventions of nine States, shall be sufficient for the Establishment of this Constitution between the States so ratifying the Same.

Done in Convention by the Unanimous Consent of the States present the Seventeenth Day of September in the Year of our Lord one thousand seven hundred and Eighty seven and of the Independence of the United States of America the Twelfth In Witness whereof We have hereunto subscribed our Names,

G？ Washington—Presidt
and deputy from Virginia

The Word, "the," being interlined between the seventh and eighth Lines of the first Page, The Word "Thirty" being partly written on an Erazure in the fifteenth Line of the first Page, The Words "is tried" being interlined between the thirty second and thirty third Lines of the first Page and the Word "the" being interlined between the forty third and forty fourth Lines of the second Page.

Attest: William Jackson Secretary

Delaware Geo: Read
Gunning Bedford Jun
John Dickinson
Richard Bassett
Jaco: Broom

Maryland James McHenry
Dan of St Thos. Jenifer
Danl. Carroll

Virginia John Blair
James Madison Jr.

North Carolina Wm. Blount
Rich'd. Dobbs Spaight
Hugh Williamson

South Carolina J. Rutledge
Charles Cotesworth Pinckney
Charles Pinckney
Pierce Butler

Georgia William Few
Abr. Baldwin

New Hampshire John Langdon
Nicholas Gilman

Massachusetts Nathaniel Gorham
Rufus King

Connecticut Wm. Saml. Johnson
Roger Sherman

New York Alexander Hamilton

New Jersey Wil: Livingston
David Brearley
Wm. Paterson
Jona: Dayton

Pennsylvania B. Franklin
Thomas Mifflin
Robt. Morris
Geo. Clymer
Thos. FitzSimons
Jared Ingersoll
James Wilson
Gouv. Morris

In Convention Monday
September 17, 1787

Present
The States of

New Hampshire, Massachusetts, Connecticut, Mr. Hamilton from New York, New Jersey, Pennsylvania, Delaware, Maryland, Virginia, North Carolina, South Carolina and Georgia.

Resolved,

That the preceding Constitution be laid before the United States in Congress assembled, and that it is the Opinion of this Convention, that it should afterwards be submitted to a Convention of Delegates, chosen in each State by the People thereof, under the Recommendation of its Legislature, for their Assent and Ratification; and that each Convention assenting to, and ratifying the Same, should give Notice thereof to the United States in Congress assembled. Resolved, That it is the Opinion of this Convention, that as soon as the Conventions of nine States shall have ratified this Constitution, the United States in Congress assembled should fix a Day on which Electors should be appointed by the States which shall have ratified the same, and a Day on which the Electors should assemble to vote for the President, and the Time and Place for commencing Proceedings under this Constitution.

That after such Publication the Electors should be appointed, and the Senators and Representatives elected: That the Electors should meet on the Day fixed for the Election of the President, and should transmit their Votes certified, signed, sealed and directed, as the Constitution requires, to the Secretary of the United States in Congress assembled, that the Senators and Representatives should convene at the Time and Place assigned; that the Senators should appoint a President of the Senate, for the sole Purpose of receiving, opening and counting the Votes for President; and, that after he shall be chosen, the Congress, together with the President, should, without Delay, proceed to execute this Constitution.

By the unanimous Order of the Convention

G? WASHINGTON—Presidt

W. JACKSON Secretary

Amendments to the Constitution of the United States of America

Articles in addition to, and Amendment of, the Constitution of the United States of America, proposed by Congress, and ratified by the several States, pursuant to the Fifth Article of the original Constitution.

Amendment I.*

Congress shall make no law respecting an establishment of religion, or prohibiting the free exercise thereof; or abridging the freedom of speech, or of the press, or the right of the people peaceably to assemble, and to petition the Government for a redress of grievances.

Amendment II.

A well regulated Militia, being necessary to the security of a free State, the right of the people to keep and bear Arms, shall not be infringed.

Amendment III.

No Soldier shall, in time of peace be quartered in any house, without the consent of the Owner, nor in time of war, but in a manner to be prescribed by law.

Amendment IV.

The right of the people to be secure in their persons, houses, papers, and effects, against unreasonable searches and seizures, shall not be violated, and no Warrants shall issue, but upon probable cause, supported by Oath or affirmation, and particularly describing the place to be searched, and the persons or things to be seized.

Amendment V.

No person shall be held to answer for a capital, or other-

---

*The first ten Amendments (Bill of Rights) were ratified effective December 15, 1791.

wise infamous crime, unless on a presentment or indictment of a Grand Jury, except in cases arising in the land or naval forces, or in the Militia, when in actual service in time of War or public danger; nor shall any person be subject for the same offence to be twice put in jeopardy of life or limb, nor shall be compelled in any criminal case to be a witness against himself, nor be deprived of life, liberty, or property, without due process of law; nor shall private property be taken for public use without just compensation.

Amendment VI.

In all criminal prosecutions, the accused shall enjoy the right to a speedy and public trial, by an impartial jury of the State and district wherein the crime shall have been committed; which district shall have been previously ascertained by law; and to be informed of the nature and cause of the accusation; to be confronted with the witnesses against him; to have compulsory process for obtaining witnesses in his favor, and to have the assistance of counsel for his defence.

Amendment VII.

In Suits at common law, where the value in controversy shall exceed twenty dollars, the right of trial by jury shall be preserved, and no fact tried by a jury shall be otherwise reexamined in any Court of the United States, than according to the rules of the common law.

Amendment VIII.

Excessive bail shall not be required, nor excessive fines imposed, nor cruel and unusual punishments inflicted.

Amendment IX.

The enumeration in the Constitution of certain rights shall not be construed to deny or disparage others retained by the people.

Amendment X.

The powers not delegated to the United States by the Constitution, nor prohibited by it to the States, are reserved to the States respectively, or to the people.

Amendment XI.*

The Judicial power of the United States shall not be construed to extend to any suit in law or equity, commenced or prosecuted against one of the United States by Citizens of another State, or by Citizens or Subjects of any Foreign State.

Amendment XII.**

The Electors shall meet in their respective states, and vote by ballot for President and Vice President, one of whom, at least, shall not be an inhabitant of the same state with themselves; they shall name in their ballots the person voted for as President, and in distinct ballots the person voted for as Vice President, and they shall make distinct lists of all persons voted for as President, and of all persons voted for as Vice President, and of the number of votes for each, which lists they shall sign and certify, and transmit sealed to the seat of the government of the United States, directed to the Presi-

---

*The Eleventh Amendment was ratified February 7, 1795.
**The Twelfth Amendment was ratified June 15, 1804.

dent of the Senate;—The President of the Senate shall, in the presence of the Senate and House of Representatives, open all the certificates and the votes shall then be counted;—The person having the greatest number of votes for President, shall be the President, if such number be a majority of the whole number of Electors appointed; and if no person have such majority, then from the persons having the highest numbers not exceeding three on the list of those voted for as President, the House of Representatives shall choose immediately, by ballot, the President. But in choosing the President, the votes shall be taken by states, the representation from each state having one vote; a quorum for this purpose shall consist of a member or members from two-thirds of the states, and a majority of all the states shall be necessary to a choice. [And if the House of Representatives shall not choose a President whenever the right of choice shall devolve upon them, before the fourth day of March next following, then the Vice President shall act as President, as in the case of the death or other constitutional disability of the President—]* The person having the greatest number of votes as Vice President, shall be the Vice President, if such number be a majority of the whole number of Electors appointed, and if no person have a majority, then from the two highest numbers on the list, the Senate shall choose the Vice President; a quorum for the purpose shall consist of two-thirds of the whole number of Senators, and a majority of the whole number shall be necessary to a choice. But no person constitutionally ineligible to the office of President shall be eligible to that of Vice President of the United States.

Amendment XIII.

Section 1. Neither slavery nor involuntary servitude, except as a punishment for crime whereof the party shall have

---

*Superseded by Section 3 of the Twentieth Amendment.

been duly convicted, shall exist within the United States, or any place subject to their jurisdiction.

Section 2. Congress shall have power to enforce this article by appropriate legislation.*

Amendment XIV.**

Section 1. All persons born or naturalized in the United States and subject to the jurisdiction thereof, are citizens of the United States and of the State wherein they reside. No State shall make or enforce any law which shall abridge the privileges or immunities of citizens of the United States; nor shall any State deprive any person of life, liberty, or property, without due process of law; nor deny to any person within its jurisdiction the equal protection of the laws.

Section 2. Representatives shall be apportioned among the several States according to their respective numbers, counting the whole number of persons in each State, excluding Indians not taxed. But when the right to vote at any election for the choice of electors for President and Vice President of the United States, Representatives in Congress, the Executive and Judicial officers of a State, or the members of the Legislature thereof, is denied to any of the male inhabitants of such State, being twenty-one years of age, and citizens of the United States, or in any way abridged, except for participation in rebellion, or other crime, the basis of representation therein shall be reduced in the proportion which the number of such male citizens shall bear to the whole number of male citizens twenty-one years of age in such State.

---

*The Thirteenth Amendment was ratified December 6, 1865.
**The Fourteenth Amendment was ratified July 9, 1868.

Section 3. No person shall be a Senator or Representative in Congress, or elector of President and Vice President, or hold any office, civil or military, under the United States, or under any State, who, having previously taken an oath, as a member of Congress, or as an officer of the United States, or as a member of any State legislature, or as an executive or judicial officer of any State, to support the Constitution of the United States, shall have engaged in insurrection or rebellion against the same, or given aid or comfort to the enemies thereof. But Congress may by a vote of two-thirds of each House, remove such disability.

Section 4. The validity of the public debt of the United States, authorized by law, including debts incurred for payment of pensions and bounties for services in suppressing insurrection or rebellion, shall not be questioned. But neither the United States nor any State shall assume or pay any debt or obligation incurred in aid of insurrection or rebellion against the United States, or any claim for the loss or emancipation of any slave; but all such debts, obligations and claims shall be held illegal and void.

Section 5. The Congress shall have power to enforce, by appropriate legislation, the provisions of this article.

Amendment XV.*

Section 1. The right of citizens of the United States to vote shall not be denied or abridged by the United States or by any State on account of race, color, or previous condition of servitude.

Section 2. The Congress shall have power to enforce this article by appropriate legislation.

---

*The Fifteenth Amendment was ratified February 3, 1870.

Amendment XVI.*

The Congress shall have power to lay and collect taxes on incomes, from whatever source derived, without apportionment among the several States, and without regard to any census or enumeration.

Amendment XVII.**

The Senate of the United States shall be composed of two Senators from each State, elected by the people thereof, for six years; and each Senator shall have one vote. The electors in each State shall have the qualifications requisite for electors of the most numerous branch of the State legislatures.

When vacancies happen in the representation of any State in the Senate, the executive authority of such State shall issue writs of election to fill such vacancies: *Provided*, That the legislature of any State may empower the executive thereof to make temporary appointments until the people fill the vacancies by election as the legislature may direct.

This amendment shall not be so construed as to affect the election or term of any Senator chosen before it becomes valid as part of the Constitution.

Amendment XVIII.***

Section 1. After one year from the ratification of this article the manufacture, sale, or transportation of intoxicating liquors within, the importation thereof into, or the exportation thereof from the United States and all territory subject

---

*The Sixteenth Amendment was ratified February 3, 1913.
**The Seventeenth Amendment was ratified April 8, 1913.
***The Eighteenth Amendment was ratified January 16, 1919. It was repealed by the Twenty-First Amendment, December 5, 1933.

to the jurisdiction thereof for beverage purposes is hereby prohibited.

Section 2. The Congress and the several States shall have concurrent power to enforce this article by appropriate legislation.

Section 3. This article shall be inoperative unless it shall have been ratified as an amendment to the Constitution by the legislatures of the several States, as provided in the Constitution, within seven years from the date of the submission hereof to the States by the Congress.

Amendment XIX.*

The right of citizens of the United States to vote shall not be denied or abridged by the United States or by any State on account of sex.

Congress shall have power to enforce this article by appropriate legislation.

Amendment XX.**

Section 1. The terms of the President and Vice President shall end at noon on the 20th day of January, and the terms of Senators and Representatives at noon on the 3d day of January, of the years in which such terms would have ended if this article had not been ratified; and the terms of their successors shall then begin.

Section 2. The Congress shall assemble at least once in every year, and such meeting shall begin at noon on the 3d day of January, unless they shall by law appoint a different day.

---

*The Nineteenth Amendment was ratified August 18, 1920.
**The Twentieth Amendment was ratified January 23, 1933.

Section 3. If, at the time fixed for the beginning of the term of the President, the President elect shall have died, the Vice President elect shall become President. If a President shall not have been chosen before the time fixed for the beginning of his term, or if the President elect shall have failed to qualify, then the Vice President elect shall act as President until a President shall have qualified; and the Congress may by law provide for the case wherein neither a President elect nor a Vice President elect shall have qualified, declaring who shall then act as President, or the manner in which one who is to act shall be selected, and such person shall act accordingly until a President or Vice President shall have qualified.

Section 4. The Congress may by law provide for the case of the death of any of the persons from whom the House of Representatives may choose a President whenever the right of choice shall have devolved upon them, and for the case of the death of any of the persons from whom the Senate may choose a Vice President whenever the right of choice shall have devolved upon them.

Section 5. Sections 1 and 2 shall take effect on the 15th day of October following the ratification of this article.

Section 6. This article shall be inoperative unless it shall have been ratified as an amendment to the Constitution by the legislatures of three-fourths of the several States within seven years from the date of its submission.

Amendment XXI.*

Section 1. The eighteenth article of amendment to the Constitution of the United States is hereby repealed.

---

*The Twenty-First Amendment was ratified December 5, 1933.

Section 2. The transportation or importation into any State, Territory, or possession of the United States for delivery or use therein of intoxicating liquors, in violation of the laws thereof, is hereby prohibited.

Section 3. This article shall be inoperative unless it shall have been ratified as an amendment to the Constitution by conventions in the several States, as provided in the Constitution, within seven years from the date of the submission hereof to the States by the Congress.

Amendment XXII.*

Section 1. No person shall be elected to the office of the President more than twice, and no person who has held the office of President, or acted as President, for more than two years of a term to which some other person was elected President shall be elected to the office of the President more than once. But this Article shall not apply to any person holding the office of President when this Article was proposed by the Congress, and shall not prevent any person who may be holding the office of President, or acting as President, during the term within which this Article becomes operative from holding the office of President or acting as President during the remainder of such term.

Section 2. This article shall be inoperative unless it shall have been ratified as an amendment to the Constitution by the legislatures of three-fourths of the several States within seven years from the date of its submission to the States by the Congress.

---

*The Twenty-Second Amendment was ratified February 27, 1951.

Amendment XXIII.*

Section 1. The District constituting the seat of Government of the United States shall appoint in such manner as the Congress may direct:

A number of electors of President and Vice President equal to the whole number of Senators and Representatives in Congress to which the District would be entitled if it were a State, but in no event more than the least populous State; they shall be in addition to those appointed by the States, but they shall be considered, for the purposes of the election of President and Vice President, to be electors appointed by a State; and they shall meet in the District and perform such duties as provided by the twelfth article of amendment.

Section 2. The Congress shall have power to enforce this article by appropriate legislation.

Amendment XXIV.**

Section 1. The right of citizens of the United States to vote in any primary or other election for President or Vice President, for electors for President or Vice President, or for Senator or Representative in Congress, shall not be denied or abridged by the United States or any State by reason of failure to pay any poll tax or other tax.

Section 2. The Congress shall have power to enforce this article by appropriate legislation.

---

*The Twenty-Third Amendment was ratified March 29, 1961.
**The Twenty-Fourth Amendment was ratified January 23, 1964.

Amendment XXV.*

Section 1. In case of the removal of the President from office or of his death or resignation, the Vice President shall become President.

Section 2. Whenever there is a vacancy in the office of the Vice President, the President shall nominate a Vice President who shall take office upon confirmation by a majority vote of both Houses of Congress.

Section 3. Whenever the President transmits to the President pro tempore of the Senate and the Speaker of the House of Representatives his written declaration that he is unable to discharge the powers and duties of his office, and until he transmits to them a written declaration to the contrary, such powers and duties shall be discharged by the Vice President as Acting President.

Section 4. Whenever the Vice President and a majority of either the principal officers of the executive departments or of such other body as Congress may by law provide, transmit to the President pro tempore of the Senate and the Speaker of the House of Representatives their written declaration that the President is unable to discharge the powers and duties of his office, the Vice President shall immediately assume the powers and duties of the office as Acting President.

Thereafter, when the President transmits to the President pro tempore of the Senate and the Speaker of the House of Representatives his written declaration that no inability exists, he shall resume the powers and duties of his office unless the Vice President and a majority of either the principal officers of the executive department or of such other body as

---

*The Twenty-Fifth Amendment was ratified February 10, 1967.

Congress may by law provide, transmit within four days to the President pro tempore of the Senate and the Speaker of the House of Representatives their written declaration that the President is unable to discharge the powers and duties of his office. Thereupon Congress shall decide the issue, assembling within forty-eight hours for that purpose if not in session. If the Congress, within twenty-one days after receipt of the latter written declaration, or, if Congress is not in session, within twenty-one days after Congress is required to assemble, determines by two-thirds vote of both Houses that the President is unable to discharge the powers and duties of his office, the Vice President shall continue to discharge the same as Acting President; otherwise, the President shall resume the powers and duties of his office.

Amendment XXVI.*

Section 1. The right of citizens of the United States, who are eighteen years of age or older, to vote shall not be denied or abridged by the United States or by any State on account of age.

Section 2. The Congress shall have power to enforce this article by appropriate legislation.

---

*The Twenty-Sixth Amendment was ratified July 1, 1971.

Important Dates

May 25, 1787: The Constitutional Convention opens as a quorum of delegates from seven states convenes in Philadelphia, to discuss revising the Articles of Confederation. Soon, representatives from 12 of the 13 states are in attendance. Rhode Island alone will not join the convention.

July 13, 1787: The Confederation Congress, meeting in New York City, passed the Northwest Ordinance with its antislavery provision, its Bill of Rights and its guarantee of religious freedom. Each of these was eventually added to the Constitution.

Sept. 17, 1787: The Constitution is approved by all 12 state delegations, and is signed by 39 of the 42 delegates present. The Convention formally adjourns.

Sept. 28, 1787: The Congress of the Confederation resolves to submit the Constitution to the states for ratification. The document is to take effect after 9 of the 13 states approve it.

Dec. 7, 1787: Delaware is the first state to ratify the Constitution. (Unanimous; 30 Yeas.)

Dec. 12, 1787: Pennsylvania becomes the second state to ratify the Constitution. (46 Yeas; 23 Nays.)

Dec. 18, 1787: New Jersey becomes the third state to ratify the Constitution. (Unanimous; 38 Yeas.)

Jan. 2, 1788: Georgia becomes the fourth state to ratify the Constitution. (Unanimous; 26 Yeas.)

Jan. 9, 1788: Connecticut becomes the fifth state to ratify the Constitution. (128 Yeas; 40 Nays.)

Feb. 6, 1788: Massachusetts becomes the sixth state to ratify the Constitution, but only after Federalists propose nine amendments, including one which would reserve to the states all powers not "expressly delegated" to the federal government by the Constitution. (187 Yeas; 168 Nays.)

April 28, 1788: Maryland becomes the seventh state to ratify the Constitution. (63 Yeas; 11 Nays.)

May 23, 1788: South Carolina becomes the eighth state to ratify the Constitution. (149 Yeas; 73 Nays.)

June 21, 1788: The Constitution becomes official when New Hampshire ratifies it, the ninth state to do so. (57 Yeas; 47 Nays.)

June 25, 1788: Virginia becomes the tenth state to ratify the Constitution, but recommends a bill of rights for American citizens. (89 Yeas; 79 Nays.)

July 26, 1788: New York becomes the 11th state to ratify the Constitution. (30 Yeas; 27 Nays.)

Feb. 4, 1789: Presidential electors select George Washington as the first President of the new government, and John Adams as the Vice President. States elect representatives and senators for the new U.S. Congress.

March 4, 1789: The first U.S. Congress convenes in New York City.

April 30, 1789: George Washington is inaugurated as the first President of the United States.

Sept. 24, 1789: Congress establishes a Supreme Court, 13 district courts, 3 circuit courts, and the position of Attorney General.

Nov. 21, 1789: North Carolina becomes the 12th state to ratify the Constitution, after Congress proposes a Bill of Rights. (194 Yeas; 77 Nays.)

May 29, 1790: Rhode Island ratifies the Constitution, the last of the original states to do so. (34 Yeas; 32 Nays.)

Dec. 15, 1791: Virginia ratifies the Bill of Rights, and the amendments become part of the U.S. Constitution.

Photo Credits